LEARN TO PLAY THE
PIANO
AND KEYBOARD

LEARN TO PLAY THE
PIANO
AND KEYBOARD

A step-by-step-guide

NICK FREETH

Bath · New York · Singapore · Hong Kong · Cologne · Delhi
Melbourne · Amsterdam · Johannesburg · Auckland · Shenzhen

This edition published by Parragon in 2012
Parragon
Queen Street House
4 Queen Street
Bath BA1 1HE, UK
www.parragon.com

Copyright © Parragon Books Ltd 2007

Designed, produced and packaged by
Stonecastle Graphics Limited

Text by Nick Freeth
Designed by Paul Turner and Sue Pressley
Edited by Philip de Ste. Croix
Diagrams by Malcolm Porter

The rights of Nick Freeth to be identified as the author of this work have been asserted in accordance with Section 77 of the Copyright, Designs and Patents Act of 1988.

All rights reserved. No part of this publication may be reproduced, stored in a retrieval system, or transmitted in any way or by any means, electronic, mechanical, photocopying, recording or otherwise, without the prior permission of the copyright holder.

ISBN 978-1-4454-7991-0
Printed in China

DVD produced by OneOneOne Productions ℗ 2007
Running time of DVD is approximately 60 minutes
Please retain packaging for future reference

Picture Credits
All photography by Exposure Images Ltd with the exception of the following: © Corbis: Michael Boys 10; Randy Duchaine 11; Alberto Martin/epa 7. © istockphoto.com: Galina Barskaya 6; Andraž Cerar 51; Compucow 16 *(above right)*; Jon Helgason 13 *(above)*; Kativ 50; Robert Rushton 4; Dustin Steller 18. Pictures on pages 12 and 15 *(below)* kindly supplied by Yamaha-Kemble Music (U.K.) Ltd.

Contents

Introduction 6

1 Choosing a keyboard 8
A brief history of the piano 10
Upright v. grand 12
Acoustic v. electronic 14
Stools and stands 16
Maintenance and technical matters 18

2 Getting started 20
Preparing to play – 1 22
Preparing to play – 2 24
Naming the notes 26
Frère Jacques – 1 28
Frère Jacques – 2 30

3 Scales and chords 32
Covering eight notes with five fingers – right hand 34
Covering eight notes with five fingers – left hand 36
Your first chords 38
Introducing the black keys 40
Transposing Frère Jacques 42

4 Introducing staff notation 44
The treble stave 46
The bass stave – and both staves together 48
Beats and bars 50
How note lengths are shown with staff notation 52
Do Ye Ken John Peel – 1 54
Do Ye Ken John Peel – 1 56

5 Co-ordinating your hands 58
Leading with the left hand 60
An extended bass riff 62
Two-handed workouts 64
Tallis's canon 66

6 Major and minor 68
Major and minor chords 70
Harmonic minor scales 72
Melodic minor scales 74
Greensleeves – 1 76
Greensleeves – 2 78

7 Putting on the style 80
The sustaining pedal 82
The 'soft' pedal and dynamic control 84
The 'three-chord trick' 86
Bluesy chords and syncopated rhythms 88
The Entertainer – 1 90
The Entertainer – 2 92
Epilog – taking it further 94

Introduction

The piano is the most enticing of instruments: if we walk into a room containing one, few of us, whether we are musicians or not, can resist pressing its keys, and it responds to even the most unskilful touch with rich, sonorous tones that contrast sharply to the rasps or squawks produced by (for example) violins or saxophones when they're tried out by beginners!

This 'user-friendliness' is also reflected in the piano's unrivaled versatility, which is largely the product of its ability to provide melodies and backings simultaneously. Though originally created for classical music, it is just as well suited to pop and jazz, and can serve as a self-contained solo voice, or as an accompaniment to other instruments and singers, either by itself or as part of a larger group. In short, it's a 'bedrock' for all kinds of music-making – perfect for everything from family sing-songs and parties to more formal onstage performances. It is frequently favored by composers and songwriters to help them work out their ideas, and endlessly useful, in both its acoustic and electronic forms, in the recording studio.

Unlocking the piano's potential

Playing the piano is a fascinating and absorbing pastime that will bring a lifetime of pleasure, and this book aims to give you a solid grounding in the techniques you'll need to get to grips with the instrument. It will also teach you how to read staff notation, help you to understand the workings of melody, harmony, and rhythm, and whet your appetite for further exploration and discovery. Just how far you decide to take your studies will, of course, be up to you; but it's undeniably true that the more effort and commitment you bring to the piano, and to music in general, the greater the rewards will be, both for you and for those with whom you share your skills. And while the process inevitably involves hard work and persistence, it will also be fun – as you'll soon realize when you begin picking out recognizable tunes and learning how to support them with suitable chords. Turn the page, and let's get started!

Opposite: The piano is perfect for supplying simple chordal backings – but equally adept at taking on more prominent musical roles.

Above: Coldplay's Chris Martin is one of many leading rock musicians who make brilliant use of the piano onstage and in the studio.

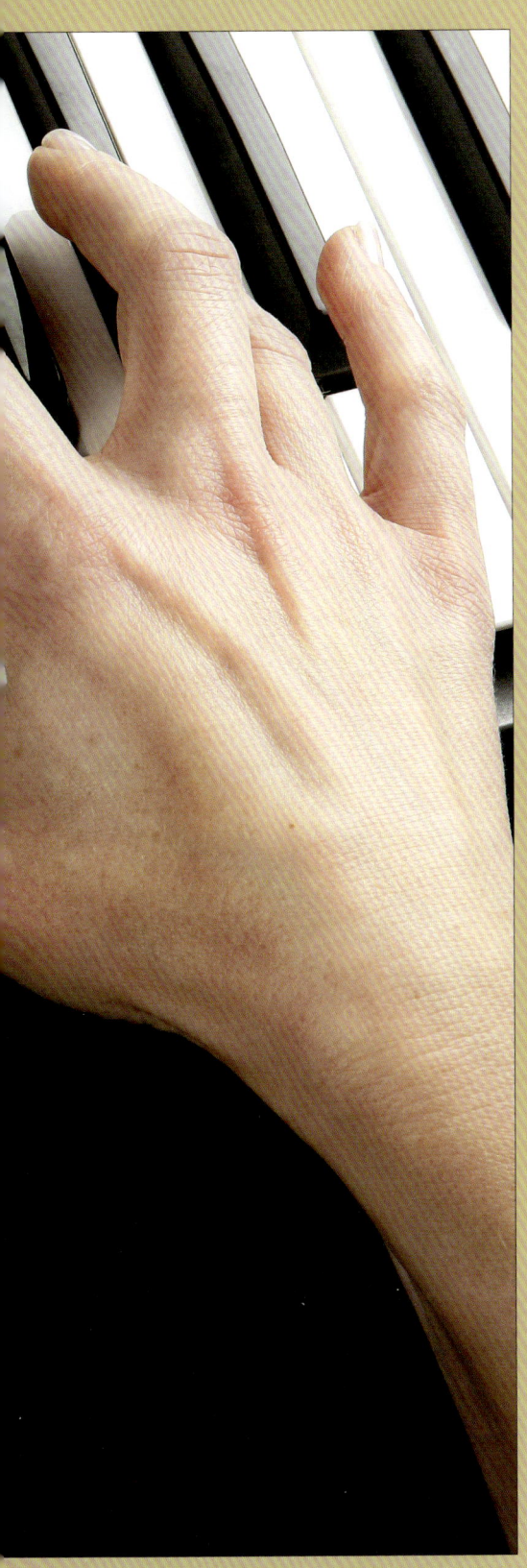

Chapter 1

Choosing a keyboard

At one time, pianos were regular items of furniture in many households, and while they're not as ubiquitous as they once were, you may be lucky enough to have a suitable instrument already standing in your living room! If not, you need to decide whether to buy or hire a traditional upright or grand, or settle instead for an electronic keyboard; most of the latter use synthesized or sampled sounds, and are currently available at surprisingly reasonable prices. This chapter will help you to choose the model that's right for you, and will also tell you a little about the history and internal workings of the piano.

A brief history of the piano

In the early 18th century, the two most popular keyboard instruments were the harpsichord, fitted with string-plucking quills, and the organ, whose keys control hinged 'pallets' that allow air into sound-generating pipes mounted on a windchest.

Harpsichords and organs cannot be made to play louder or softer by touching their keyboards more heavily or gently, but in about 1709, an Italian, Bartolomeo Cristofori, introduced what he called a '*gravicembalo col piano e forte*' – literally, a 'harpsichord with soft and loud'; it replaced the standard harpsichord's quills with hammers that responded to harder or lighter keyboard pressure, enabling performers to produce subtle gradations of volume and tone.

This early type of piano (often called a 'fortepiano') provided a smaller range of notes and a less powerful timbre than the modern 'pianoforte', which emerged, in the wake of various transitional designs, during the 19th century. By the 1850s, sales of the newer instrument (especially in its space-saving 'upright' form) were booming, and cast iron, rather than wood, was being widely used to construct pianos' load-bearing frames. The extra strength supplied by the metal was soon to be essential, as, within a few decades, the heavier, richer sounding strings increasingly favored by manufacturers were subjecting a typical 88-note concert grand to tensions totaling some 20 tons – a figure matched, and sometimes exceeded, by today's pianos!

Above: Even though this elegant harpsichord has two keyboards, enabling players to combine different tonal settings, the palette of sounds it provides is more limited than the piano's.

Opposite: One of the many magnificent concert grand pianos produced by the famous firm of Steinway & Sons, founded by German-born New Yorker Henry E. Steinway in 1853.

Upright v. grand

Unlike other musicians, who can put their chosen instrument away in a cupboard or even a drawer when it isn't being used, you'll have to share your living space with your piano – and traditional (non-electronic) models can be dauntingly large.

Grand pianos have their strings and hammers mounted horizontally in a wooden casing with a lid that can be raised to maximize the instrument's sonic projection. Most grands are a little under 5ft (1.5m) wide at their keyboard end, but their length varies considerably. A 'baby grand' is about 4ft 11in to 5ft 6in (1.49–1.68m) long (smaller, 'petite' grands are also available), while a full-size 'concert grand' measures up to 9ft (2.75m).

A good grand will feel, sound, and look superb, but is very expensive – a new 'baby' may cost well over $10,000 – and won't be heard to its best advantage unless it's placed in a big room.

Above: Grand pianos – even 'baby' grands like the one illustrated here – may be difficult to accommodate in smaller sized homes, but they are the undoubted aristocrats of the keyboard world.

CHOOSING A KEYBOARD

A more compact solution

For many of us, **upright** pianos are a better bet for domestic use. Due to the vertical positioning of their strings and action, and the slight muffling effect of their cases, their response and sound will always be inferior to a grand's, but for learning and practice purposes, these drawbacks are more than outweighed by convenience and relative affordability. An upright's keyboard is the same size as a grand's, while the height of its casing is typically a little over 4ft (1.22m), though 'studio' or 'console' models can be found that are somewhat lower.

Above: A traditional upright piano with a matching stool. The casing on some modern uprights is more compact than that seen on this model.

Right: Piano strings are made from steel wire: the thicker bass ones are encased in copper wrappings, while their higher pitched counterparts are left bare.

Acoustic v. electronic

*If space and cash are at a premium, there are several viable alternatives to regular, acoustic pianos. One inexpensive solution is to buy an **all-purpose electronic keyboard** with integral loudspeakers.*

Most of these offer a plethora of digitally produced sounds, including imitations of various types of piano, and also feature onboard audio effects and other 'bells and whistles.' However, their keys are sometimes lightweight and flimsy, and though all but the cheapest models provide 'touch sensitivity' (responding to heavier or more gentle playing with louder or quieter notes and chords), they rarely come close to matching the subtle response that can be evoked from a real piano.

The synthesized piano tones in such units (often generated artificially from various combinations of audio waveforms) tend not to be very convincing either, and better results can be obtained with electronic keyboards that use **samples** – actual recordings – of acoustic pianos. If you have a suitable computer, you can purchase software containing these sounds, and access them using an external keyboard like the one in our pictures. There's more information about doing this on pages 18-19.

Below: E-MU's Xboard 49 is a moderately priced electronic keyboard controller, designed to play sounds supplied from software or other outboard devices.

CHOOSING A KEYBOARD

However, a dedicated **electronic piano**, with samples, keyboard, and (usually) a loudspeaker system all built in, may be a preferable, though more expensive, option: Yamaha, Roland, and other companies make fine, relatively compact instruments of this type, with keyboards that replicate the feel of an acoustic grand, and (on some models) elegant finishes similar to a traditional piano's.

Left: Though lightweight, the Xboard 49's keys are full-size, highly responsive, and robust enough to withstand reasonably heavy use.

Above: This Yamaha CLP Clavinova offers digitally sampled sounds, and boasts an **88-note keyboard** whose touch closely resembles that of an acoustic piano.

CHOOSING A KEYBOARD

Stools and stands

It's essential to be comfortable at the piano – and taking time and care over choosing a suitable seat for your instrument will not only prevent aches and pains, but help to ensure that your playing technique develops correctly.

For most pianists, the traditional stool or bench supplied with many standard uprights and grands is ideal, as it's well padded, stable, and usually adjustable. Being able to raise or lower the stool is handy because, when sitting down to play, your arms should be roughly parallel to the floor, and since you can't reposition the keyboard on a regular piano to achieve this, you may need to alter the elevation of your seat instead. If you're stuck with a fixed-height stool that's too low, you can, of course, resort to cushions (or even telephone directories!) to bring yourself up to the correct level; if it's too high, however, you'll need to replace it.

A few performers prefer to use a chair at the piano; try this by all means, but make sure you select an upright, dining table-type seat with a substantial frame and, most crucially, no arms to get in your way.

Left: The side-mounted knob on this classic-style stool makes precise height adjustment quick and easy.

Above: With its leather-covered seat and elegantly shaped legs, the stool perfectly complements the grand piano.

CHOOSING A KEYBOARD

Above: Having correctly set and positioned your stool, you'll be relaxed and at ease at the piano, and able to practice enjoyably and without strain.

If you're playing a keyboard without legs, such as the one described and illustrated on the previous two pages, you should purchase an adjustable stand for it; this will allow you to set the height of the unit relative to your chosen seat. It isn't advisable to try to play standing up until you're a little more experienced.

Above: Metal, X-shaped keyboard stands are not exactly things of beauty – but they are functional, robust, and inexpensive.

Maintenance and technical matters

When calculating the overall cost of acquiring a piano, bear in mind that both uprights and grands should receive regular maintenance by trained technicians.

Above: A piano tuner at work on a concert grand. All stringed keyboards require fairly frequent maintenance to keep them in peak condition.

If you purchase your own instrument, you'll have to budget for this; if you hire or 'hire to buy' an instrument, it may be possible to arrange for servicing as part of the rental package.

The most frequent adjustment required by an acoustic piano is, of course, tuning: a grand in a major concert hall will have its string pitches checked and corrected before every performance, and most manufacturers recommend that home pianos should be tuned at least every six months. Keys, dampers, and other components also need occasional attention – though many of the problems that afflict them can be avoided by carefully regulating the temperature (which should be between about 65 and 70°F/18 and 21°C) and humidity in the room where the piano is installed.

Synthesizers and sampler-based electronic instruments never go out of tune, and rarely suffer mechanical breakdowns. However, their complex circuitry may sometimes malfunction, and can be severely damaged by spilled fluids (especially sticky drinks) and rough handling. When shopping for an electronic keyboard, look for one that has a minimum of 49 notes, and keys the same size as an acoustic piano's; if you've decided to use a keyboard in conjunction with a computer, as described on pages 14-15, you will need a MIDI (musical instrument digital interface) connecter to link it to your PC. Your electronic instrument's sound source, whether built-in or supplied from software, should have at least '12-note polyphony;' in other words, it must be capable of playing a minimum of 12 notes simultaneously. This figure will be substantially exceeded by more expensive keyboards.

Above: The rear panel of the E-MU Xboard 49 includes a 5-pin MIDI socket; this, and the adjacent USB port, can be used to connect the keyboard to a computer.

Right: Many of the 88 notes on a concert grand are produced by groups of three or two strings set to the same pitch. The drift in their tuning that occurs inevitably over time can eventually, if not corrected by regular adjustment, make even the finest piano sound like a cheap 'honky-tonk.'

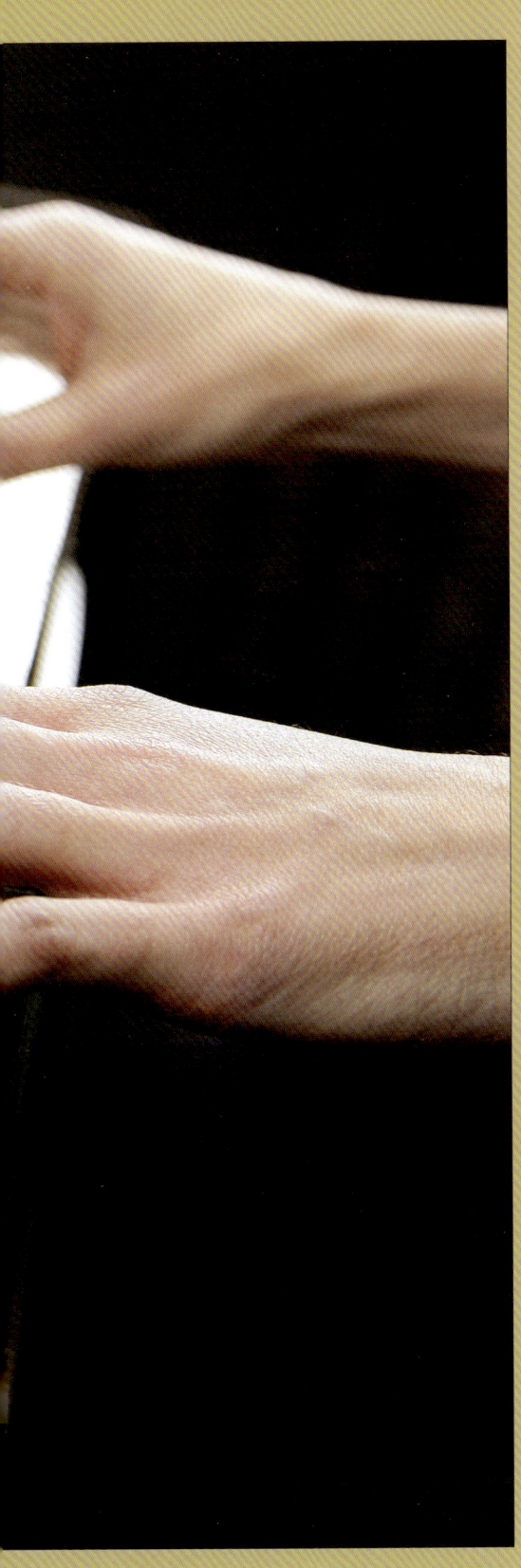

Chapter 2
Getting started

Now you've acquired a suitable keyboard, it's time to take the first steps toward playing it. There are a few conventions and technicalities to familiarize yourself with first: the next few pages explain how pianists identify and number their fingers, how to place your hands correctly on the instrument, and how to find and keep your musical bearings when confronted by its initially bewildering array of black and white keys. Once you've absorbed this information, you'll be ready to learn your first tune – and to try performing it both as a solo melody, and with a simple accompaniment provided by your left hand.

GETTING STARTED

Preparing to play – 1

Before you sit down to play for the first time, take a moment to examine the layout of your keyboard. It's made up of a continuous line of white keys, with groups of two and three thinner and shorter black keys set between them in a recurring pattern.

Every key, when pressed, produces a musical note to which we give an alphabetical name. Just for now, we're only concerned with one of these notes: C. There are, in fact, quite a number of Cs on the keyboard; wherever there's a group of two black keys, the white key immediately to the left of the first black key is always a C (see diagram). Put your right hand out, find each of the C keys on your keyboard – starting at its left end, and moving upward – and press them down, one after the other, with a finger or thumb. Those nearest the bottom of the keyboard will be lower in pitch, and as you move upward, the Cs you play will sound higher…but they should all closely resemble one another; if they don't, check that you've correctly identified the keys producing them!

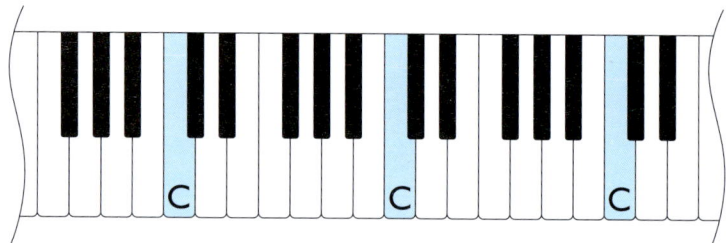

Now stand about half-way along the keyboard, put your right hand out, and locate the C nearest to you: this note is known as 'middle C,' and will serve as a focal point for much of your playing. Get your stool or chair, position it more-or-less opposite middle C, and sit down.

Below: Don't be daunted by this expanse of keys: once you're familiar with their layout, you'll be able to find the notes you need virtually instantly.

GETTING STARTED

Left: Middle C, held down here with the right hand thumb, is an essential reference point. Having located it, you can begin 'navigating' around the rest of the keyboard.

Below: On an 88-note piano like this one, middle C is always the 40th key from the left. Its position differs when the keyboard is shorter: on a narrower 49-note instrument, for example, it will be the 25th key from the bottom.

GETTING STARTED

Preparing to play – 2

Study the photographs opposite, and copy the positions they demonstrate to ensure you're seated correctly at the keyboard. As explained on pages 16-17, the height of your stool or chair should be set so that your arms are parallel to the ground.

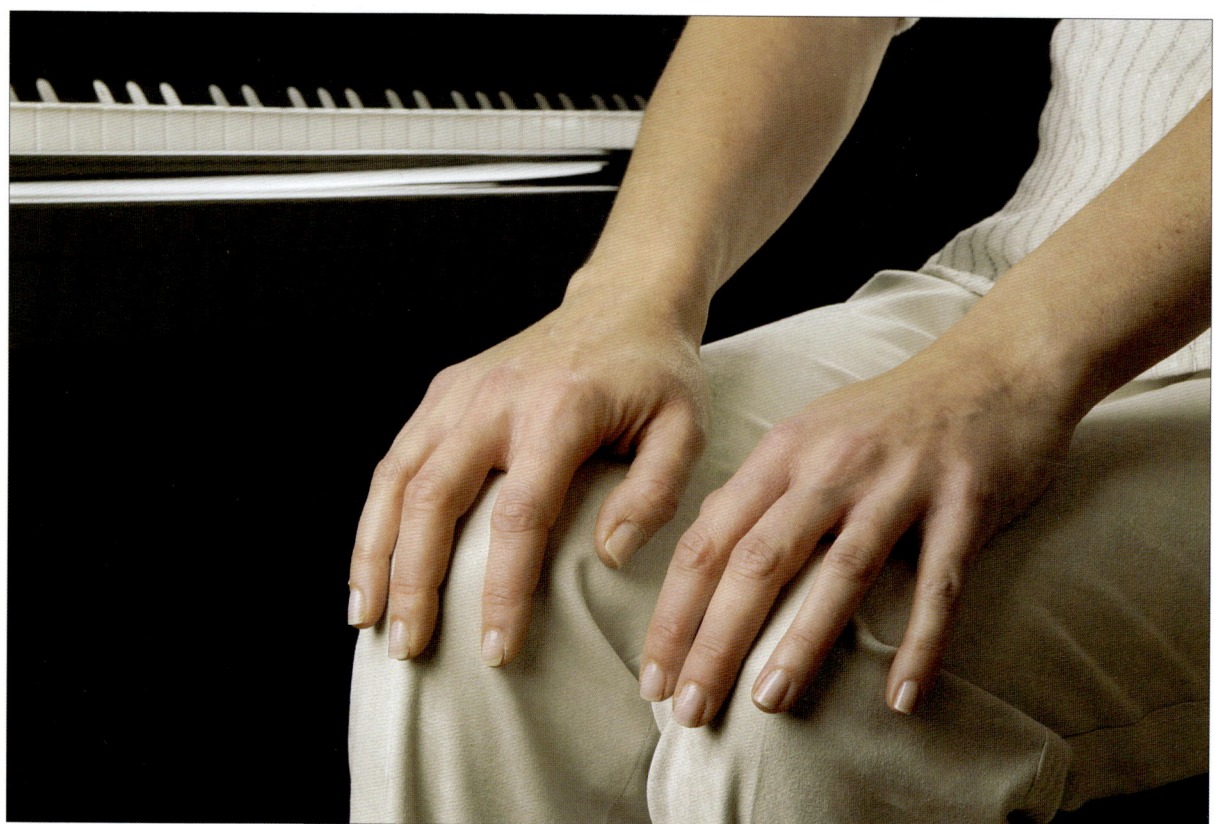

It's also important to keep your body upright but relaxed, and to rest your feet firmly on the floor – not on the piano's pedals!

Let's focus now on your hands. Pianists use all ten digits when they play, sometimes fingering successions of notes to create a tune, and sometimes making chords by pressing down several keys at once. Whichever you're doing, it's essential that your hands should be **arched**, as though you had a ball beneath each of your palms. Holding them like this compensates for the differing lengths of your fingers and thumbs, minimizes stress, and produces a better, more even tone. NEVER strike the keys with flat fingers – it's a recipe for musical and muscular disaster!

You can form your hands into an arched shape by resting them on your kneecaps and gripping slightly; having done this, place them on the keyboard as shown in the photograph, with

Above: Arching your hands to play will soon become second nature to you – but until it does, your knees can serve as a convenient 'mold' for them!

your right hand thumb on middle C, and the little finger of your left hand on the C exactly 7 white notes below it. Press down middle C fairly firmly with your right hand thumb, then sound the four white notes immediately above it, one after the other, with your curved fingers. Try this several times, and then perform the same exercise with your left hand, starting with its little finger on C, and then using each of the other digits in turn.

Below: As the left hand's little finger strikes the C that lies seven white notes beneath middle C, its other digits, all suitably arched, prepare to play the four adjacent 'ivories,' one at a time.

Right: Middle C, and the four white keys above it, should be easily reachable with your right hand. If necessary, adjust your seat by moving it slightly inward or outward for maximum comfort.

GETTING STARTED

Naming the notes

For obvious reasons, patterns of notes like the one you've just played are called 'five finger exercises.' They're useful to help you get the feel of the keyboard, and it's well worth repeating the routine on pages 24-25 with each hand until it's second nature.

While practicing it, try varying the speed and the volume, and reversing the direction of the notes, going downward (toward C) as well as upward. Remember to keep your hands arched as you play the notes.

Having mastered the exercise, you need to be able to put names to all the notes comprising it; once you've done this, you can follow instructions telling you how to combine them (and other notes you haven't encountered yet) into a proper melody, not merely an ascending and descending sequence of pitches. You're already familiar with C: the white note immediately above it in the exercise is called D, and the next three white keys are, predictably enough, named E, F, and G.

Beyond G, however, are two white notes you haven't had to use yet, and the name of the first of them may cause some confusion: it isn't H, as you might have expected, but A. To its immediate right is (you guessed it!) B; and the following note is, logically enough, C. This won't come as a surprise to you, as you already know, from pages 22-23, that the C key is always found immediately to the left of a group of two black keys.

These patterns of note-names recur all the way along the piano, so we've now identified all its white keys. We'll examine the black ones later, but first, let's put all this knowledge to practical use by learning a real tune.

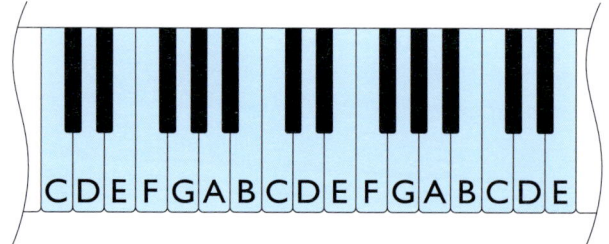

Right: The key being pressed down here is E; it's located two white keys above middle C, on which the thumb is resting.

Left: Here the index finger of the left hand strikes F, three white keys (and four note names) above C.

Below: The right hand's index finger is poised above G, while the next finger prepares to play A, and the remaining digits are in position over (respectively) B and C.

GETTING STARTED

Frère Jacques – 1

The seven letters representing the piano's white keys are often used to create easy-to-read lists of the notes that make up simple tunes. Over the next few pages, you'll be learning how to play a melody from one of these, and also finding out how numbers can be combined with it to show suitable fingerings.

The nursery rhyme *Frère Jacques* has been chosen as our first tune because you're almost certain to know it (this is important, as setting the details of an unfamiliar melody down on paper is not easy unless we can employ musical notation – which you haven't learned yet!), and because it falls fairly easily under the fingers, using all but one of the notes from A to G to which you've just been introduced.

Let's begin with your right hand on its own. Place it on the keyboard with your thumb on middle C, and the other fingers on, respectively, D, E, F, and G (see photograph below); these notes are all you'll need to play the first two lines of *Frère Jacques*. Here they are, set out in a three-decker 'list'. The song's lyrics are at the bottom, the note-names that go with them are in the middle, and the top line indicates the fingering you should use to play the notes. Pianists always use the figure 1 to represent the thumb, while the other digits (index to little) are assigned in sequence the numbers 2, 3, 4, and 5 (see diagram).

Practice this (slowly at first) until you can play it smoothly and steadily; when you're ready to go on, turn the page and we'll look at what happens in the second part of the tune.

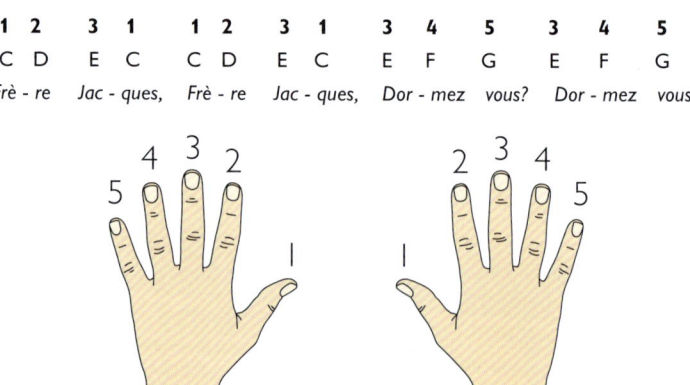

1	2	3	1	1	2	3	1	3	4	5	3	4	5
C	D	E	C	C	D	E	C	E	F	G	E	F	G
Frè -	re	Jac -	ques,	Frè -	re	Jac -	ques,	Dor -	mez	vous?	Dor -	mez	vous?

Right: The right hand thumb has just played the first note (C) in line one of *Frère Jacques*; now finger 2 sounds the D that follows it.

GETTING STARTED

Right: E is used on the first syllable of the word 'Jacques' in the song; here it's sounded by finger 3.

Below: We've now reached the 'vous' of 'Dormez vous?'. The note for this syllable is a G, assigned to finger 5.

GETTING STARTED

Frère Jacques – 2

The second section of Frère Jacques *involves some new fingerings, and (at the end of the song) a change of hand position.*

The line 'Sonnez les matines' requires the following notes –

G A G F E C
Son - nez les ma - ti - nes

– but how is your right hand going to reach the A, which lies beyond the G you've been playing with your little finger (numbered 5)? The solution is to alter the fingering for this line, sounding the G with finger 4, then using your 5th on the A (see photograph), your 3rd on F, and your 2nd on E. Your thumb plays middle C as before.

4	5	4	3	2	1	4	5	4	3	2	1
G	A	G	F	E	C	G	A	G	F	E	C
Son -	nez	les	ma -	ti -	nes,	Son -	nez	les	ma -	ti -	nes,

The song's final line imitates the sound of the bells that Frère Jacques should be ringing, using middle C, and the G three white keys below it – not the higher-pitched G you've played previously. The easiest way to get to this lower note is to strike it with your thumb, and, just for once, assign middle C to finger 4 (see photograph at the top of page 31).

Right: The right hand's digits have been repositioned, and finger 4 has just struck the G for the 'Son-' of 'Sonnez les matines' in *Frère Jacques*. Finger 5 now plays the next note, A (given to the syllable '-nez').

GETTING STARTED

Left: A new hand and finger placement: the right hand's thumb plays the low G ('Dang'), and the 4th prepares to sound middle C ('Dong').

Below: The syllable 'Dor-' of 'Dormez vous?', performed with two hands: the left's finger 5 provides a C, accompanying the E supplied by finger 3 of the right hand.

4	1	4	4	1	4
C	low G	C	C	low G	C
Ding,	Dang,	Dong,	Ding,	Dang,	Dong

It'll take a little time to get used to these new fingerings – but keep working at them and they'll eventually fall into place, and you'll be ready to perform *Frère Jacques* in full. Here's the complete song: you can play it as a solo right hand melody, or combine it with a simple accompaniment from your left hand, which should strike and hold down a C (using finger 5 – see photograph) at the start of each line.

1	2	3	1	1	2	3	1	3	4	5	3	4	5
C	D	E	C	C	D	E	C	E	F	G	E	F	G
Frè-	re	Jac-	ques,	Frè-	re	Jac-	ques,	Dor-	mez	vous?	Dor-	mez	vous?

4	5	4	3	2	1	4	5	4	3	2	1	4	1	4	4	1	4
G	A	G	F	E	C	G	A	G	F	E	C	C	low G	C	C	low G	C
Son-	nez	les	ma-	ti-	nes,	Son-	nez	les	ma-	ti-	nes,	Ding,	Dang,	Dong,	Ding,	Dang,	Dong

Chapter 3

Scales and chords

Over the next few pages, we'll be unlocking more of the piano's possibilities, as you learn fingering techniques that will enable you to move around the keyboard with greater ease and fluency. We'll also be turning our attention to chords – the combinations of notes that are essential for accompanying melodies and enriching the sound of your playing.

And, at the end of this chapter, we begin to make use of the piano's black keys, in a process that will open up broader musical horizons, allowing you to get to grips with tunes rooted on notes other than C.

SCALES AND CHORDS

Covering eight notes with five fingers – right hand

The Frère Jacques *tune used a total of seven notes (including two Gs), and you had to adjust the position of your five right hand digits to play them all. Let's now look at a way of covering eight notes smoothly and easily with one hand.*

Strike middle C with your right hand thumb, then sound the adjacent D with finger 2, followed by E with finger 3. You could now reach F and G with (respectively) digits 4 and 5 – but having done so, there'd be no fingers available for the notes beyond G, and you'd be obliged to reposition your hand in order to continue up the keyboard. Fortunately, there's a simple solution to this problem; instead of playing F with your 4th finger, use your thumb instead, passing it under finger 3 to do so. After completing this maneuver, you'll find that fingers 2, 3, 4, and 5 are perfectly placed for G, A, B, and C, and, with a little practice, you should be able to play the eight notes upward from middle C – the technical term for such a sequence is a **scale** – swiftly and smoothly. The secret to achieving a seamless transition from note to note lies in keeping your fingers fairly close to the keys, and having each digit ready to play a little before it's needed, so that you can sound the next note as soon as you release the previous one.

For a downward scale ending on middle C, you'll need to finger as indicated below:

5	4	3	2	1	3	2	1
C	B	A	G	F	E	D	C

As you can see, the 'crossover' here occurs between F and E, where finger 3 traverses the thumb to reach E; this movement brings digits 2 and 1 into position for D and C.

Above: Finger 2 plays note two (D) of the ascending scale that began on middle C. Digit 3 is already in position over the E that will be required next.

SCALES AND CHORDS

Left: When going upward, the thumb crosses under finger 3 to sound F; the same maneuver occurs in reverse during the downward scale, with the 3rd digit passing over the thumb onto E.

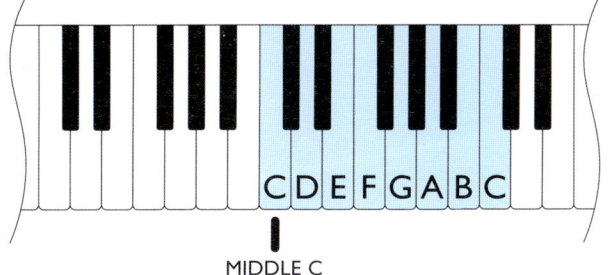

MIDDLE C

Below: A simple left hand accompaniment (the C below middle C, supplied by finger 5) adds some additional musical interest to the straightforward up-and-down scale of C being played above it.

SCALES AND CHORDS

Covering eight notes with five fingers – left hand

Your left hand has had a fairly easy time of it recently, but will need to develop the same ability as the right to cope with scales and other successions of notes.

Let's start putting it through its paces, using the same C to C exercise we featured on the previous two pages.

Place the 5th (little) finger of your left hand on the C seven white keys below middle C, and play the first five notes of an ascending scale (C, D, E, F, and G) with digits 5, 4, 3, 2, and 1 (thumb). You now have no further 'spare' fingers – until you cross your 3rd finger over your thumb, as shown in the photograph; strike A with the 3rd, and complete the scale with B and middle C sounded, respectively, by your 2nd finger and thumb.

Practice the scale until you feel confident; mastering it may require a good deal of repetition, as you haven't used your left hand in this way before. Once the notes are sounding steady and fluent, try playing the scale in reverse (downward from middle C), beginning with your left hand thumb, and 2nd and 3rd fingers, then passing your thumb under the 3rd to reach G (see photograph), and finishing the sequence with your four other fingers.

To help you practice these rising and descending scales, here are all the left hand fingerings for them, set out in table form:

```
       5 4 3 2 1 3 2 1
(up)   C D E F G A B C

       1 2 3 1 2 3 4 5
(down) C B A G F E D C
```

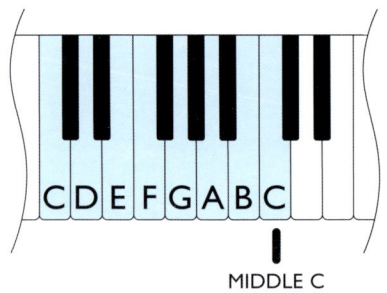

Below: The transition from the fifth to the sixth note of a rising C scale: the left hand's finger 3 passes over the thumb to get to A.

SCALES AND CHORDS

Left: Going downward from A to G. As finger 3 strikes the higher note, the thumb prepares to play G, 'setting up' the remaining digits to complete the rest of the scale smoothly.

Below: Home again – but having made it down to the C below middle C, why not change direction and head upward again, using finger 4 (on D), finger 3 (on E) and so on?

SCALES AND CHORDS

Your first chords

The ease with which the piano can combine melodies and chords sets it apart from most other instruments; let's take advantage of its capabilities by learning two easy, three-note chords (known as 'triads') and using them as a simple accompaniment for a scale.

Rest the little finger of your left hand on the C below middle C, then place your 3rd finger and thumb on, respectively, E and G (see photograph). Now lift your hand about half an inch above the keyboard, and bring its three fingers down on these three notes, sounding them simultaneously and with equal pressure. Practice this until it feels comfortable, then try a second chord – comprising G, B, and D, as shown on the diagram opposite – with the same fingers.

Next, use your right hand's thumb, 3rd, and 5th fingers to strike the same chords a little higher up the keyboard: the diagram and photographs will guide you toward the required notes (C-E-G and G-B-D) if you aren't sure where to find them.

Once you've become accustomed to the unfamiliar sensations of chord-playing, see if you can play an ascending C to C scale with one hand, while 'backing' it with the C-E-G and G-B-D triads. The tables in the next column set out the fingerings, and tell you where and when to sound the chords. Good luck!

RIGHT HAND: SCALE/LEFT HAND: CHORDS

RH FINGER	1	2	3	1	2	3	4	5
RH NOTE	C	D	E	F	G	A	B	C
	|			|			|	
LH CHORDS	C/E/G	—		G/B/D	—		C/E/G	*(play chords with fingers 5, 3, and 1)*

LEFT HAND: SCALE/RIGHT HAND: CHORDS

RH CHORDS	C/E/G	—		G/B/D	—		C/E/G	*(play chords with fingers 1, 3, and 5)*
	|			|			|	
LH FINGER	5	4	3	2	1	3	2	1
LH NOTE	C	D	E	F	G	A	B	C

Right: The left hand plays a C triad, fingered by 5 (on C itself), 3 (E), and 1 (G). Keep your fingers arched as you strike these three notes!

SCALES AND CHORDS

Left: The three-note chord of G should fall just as easily under your left hand digits as the one of C you've just mastered.

Below: The right hand tackles a G chord, with the thumb on G, and the notes B and D fingered (respectively) by 3 and 5.

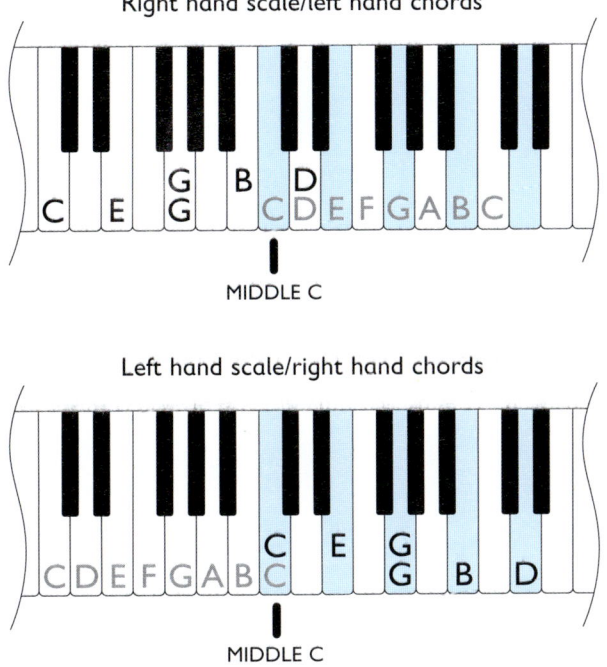

SCALES AND CHORDS

Introducing the black keys

So far, we've focused exclusively on the piano's white keys, but now it's time to investigate the 'ebonies' that separate some of them, and, in the process, learn a little more about the structure of the scales you've been playing.

As you'll have noticed, there are black keys between each of the piano's white ones, with the exception of E and F and B and C. To hear the notes they provide, strike middle C with your right hand thumb, move on to the black note immediately to its right, then continue up the keyboard as far as the next C, using the fingering set out below (*bl* stands for 'black key'):

1 3 1 3 1 2 3 1 3 1 3 1 2
C bl D bl E F bl G bl A bl B C

What you've just played is a *chromatic scale*, and the difference in pitch between each of its steps is a *semitone* – the narrowest *interval* (distance between notes) that the piano can provide. Let's see how this scale relates to a standard 8-note one, so that we can discover exactly how the latter is built up.

As the diagram below left reveals, our regular C to C scale has 2-semitone (= 1 tone) gaps separating its first and second, second and third, fourth and fifth, fifth and sixth, and sixth and seventh degrees (C to D, D to E, F to G, G to A, and A to B), and spaces of a single semitone between E and F and B and C (notes 3-4 and 7-8). Applying this formula, and deploying the piano's black keys where necessary, enables us to create 8-note scales with identical intervals starting from any note we choose – a procedure which, as you're about to find out, can help to breathe new life into familiar tunes…

Below: This chromatic scale feels and sounds very different to the 8-note scale patterns rooted on C you've learned previously. Finger 3 is used for all its black notes.

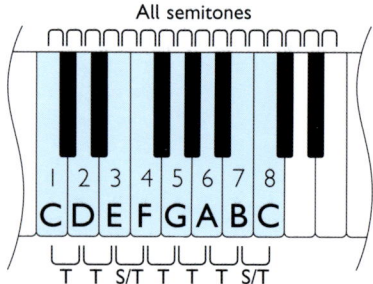

SCALES AND CHORDS

Left: A little higher up our chromatic scale, the right hand's finger 2 strikes F as the thumb releases E; the 3rd, meanwhile, is in place for the next black key.

Right: The transition from a black to a white note: when the 3rd finger releases the 'ebony,' the 2nd will be in position to sound the C a semitone above the B assigned to the thumb.

SCALES AND CHORDS

Transposing Frère Jacques

The scale and 'home note' on which a tune is rooted define what musicians call the piece's **key**.

The version of *Frère Jacques* featured on pages 28-31 was in the key of C – but here we're going to **transpose** it (to use another new technical term!) to F, and give it a new left hand accompaniment.

First, let's master a basic scale starting on F. The piano keys needed to play it, shown in the diagram opposite, are all white except the one producing the scale's fourth note, for which we use the 'ebony' immediately to the right of the A that supplies the scale's third step. Black keys, and the notes they provide, share the letters of their 'ivory' neighbors, combined with

a suffix – 'sharp' (#) or 'flat' (♭) denoting whether the black note is higher or lower than the white one from which it takes its name. The 'ebony' we're concerned with lies a semitone below B, and is therefore called **B flat** (B♭).

This is a right hand fingering diagram for the new scale. It begins on the F located three white notes above middle C; after striking B♭, pass your thumb beneath finger 4 to reach the remaining notes.

1	2	3	4	1	2	3	4
F	G	A	B♭	C	D	E	F

Above: B♭, the fourth step of the scale of F, is struck by the 4th finger of the right hand, while the thumb moves below the finger into position on C (see diagram below).

Frère Jaques in the key of F

Now here's the transposed version of *Frère Jacques* – also with some new fingerings!

1	2	3	1	1	2	3	1	3	4	5	3	4	5
F	G	A	F	F	G	A	F	A	B♭	C	A	B♭	C
Frè -	re	Jac -	ques,	Frè -	re	Jac -	ques,	Dor -	mez	vous?	Dor -	mez	vous?

4	5	4	3	2	1	4	5	4	3	2	1	4	1	4	4	1	4
C	D	C	B♭	A	F	C	D	C	B♭	A	F	F	C*	F	F	C*	F
Son -	nez	les	ma -	ti -	nes,	Son -	nez	les	ma -	ti -	nes,	Ding,	Dang,	Dong,	Ding,	Dang,	Dong

* – the C here is 'middle C'

To flesh out the melody, use your left hand to play a 'drone' comprising F and C – see photograph below. Strike this at the start of each line, keeping the keys held down to allow the notes to ring.

The structure of the F scale

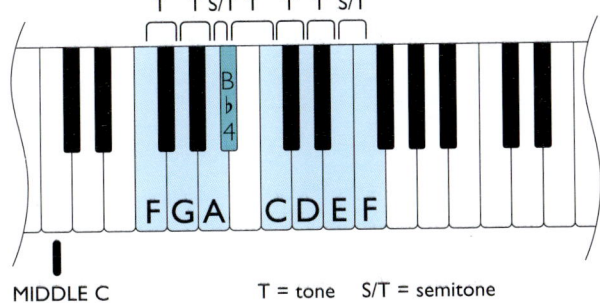

Above: A new note for *Frère Jacques*. Here, finger 4 plays the B♭ for the '-mez' of 'Dormez vous?'

Left: Another B♭ – this one sounded by the right hand's 3rd finger on the syllable 'ma-' of 'Sonnez les matines,' while the left hand supplies its F/C bass drone.

Chapter 4
Introducing staff notation

The diagrams and lists of notes you've been using to play so far are very limited in what they can communicate about a piece of music. They can't, for example, convey its rhythm, or even show chords properly; and now that you've developed sufficient technical skills to perform more demanding and complex material than scales and nursery rhymes, it's essential that you learn to read **staff notation** – the standard method used by composers to write down and share their work. Accordingly, this chapter provides a crash course in what some musicians call 'the dots.' Don't be discouraged if you struggle with them to start with: those initially mysterious squiggles and symbols will soon give up their secrets!

INTRODUCING STAFF NOTATION

The treble stave

*Music for the piano is written down on two groups of five lines called **staves**. The top stave (sometimes also spelled 'staff') carries the notes played by the right hand, while the lower one is used for a piece's left hand part. Let's start by finding out how the upper (or **treble**) stave works.*

The lines and spaces on a stave represent musical pitches: we can discover which line or space refers to which note by looking at the **clef** symbol that appears at the start of each stave. The upper stave features a **treble** (or **G**) **clef**, curled round the second line of the stave: its presence tells us that this line stands for the G four white notes above middle C. It's now relatively easy to work out the locations of all the other notes on the stave: the four spaces between its five lines correspond (respectively) to F, A, C (the one seven white keys above middle C), and E, while the five lines represent E, G, B, D, and F (see notation and diagram).

Musical notes are also placed below the lowest stave line, and beyond its top one: the position immediately above the highest (F) line stands for G, while the D one note above middle C appears just below the bottom (E) line. Middle C itself doesn't fit onto the treble clef's 'regular' lines and spaces, and is written below the stave, using a short, horizontal line known as a 'ledger line.' Ledger lines can also be used for other notes lying above or beneath the stave (see notation).

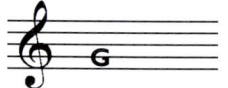

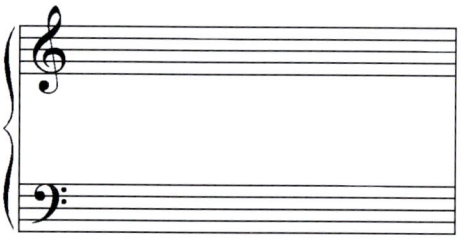

Below: The little finger of the right hand sounds the 'G clef G.' The note would be written on the stave line that is curled around by the treble clef.

INTRODUCING STAFF NOTATION

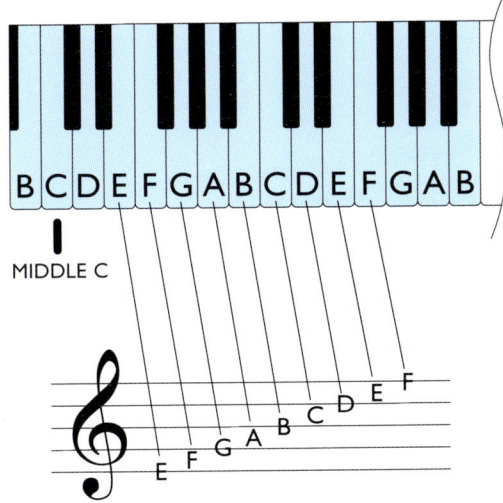

Right: The E being played here by the thumb would appear on the lowest line of the treble stave.

Below: This high-pitched A (the third note from the right in the notation below right) lies above the range of the five standard stave lines, and is therefore notated using a ledger line.

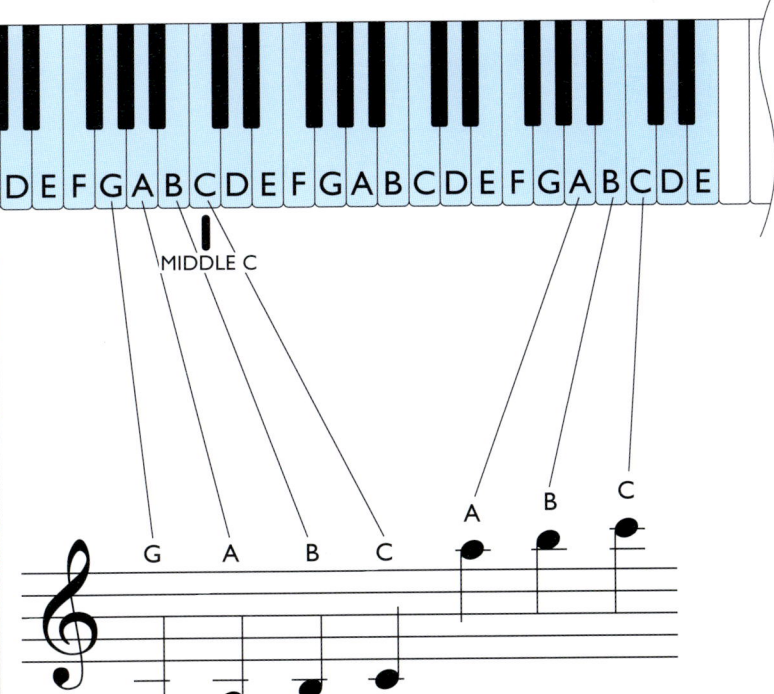

INTRODUCING STAFF NOTATION

The bass stave – and both staves together

The lower of the two staves used for piano music has the same five lines and four spaces as the upper one – but because it carries another clef sign, the musical pitches these 'stand for' are quite different to those on the treble stave.

The clef in question is called a **bass** (or '**F**') **clef**; it curls around the second of the five lines on the stave (counting downward), indicating that it represents F – specifically, the F four white notes below middle C (see diagram). Knowing the position of this note, we can figure out that the five lines on the bass stave (counting, once again, from the top) equate to A, F (obviously!), D, B, and G, and that its spaces correspond to G, E, C, and A. The one point of similarity between the clefs lies in their placement of middle C, as you can see from the notation opposite…though in the bass clef, the ledger line standing for it appears above the stave – rather than below it, as in the treble.

To help you familiarize yourself with the treble and bass staves, here's an easily recognizable sequence of pitches – a scale of C – set out

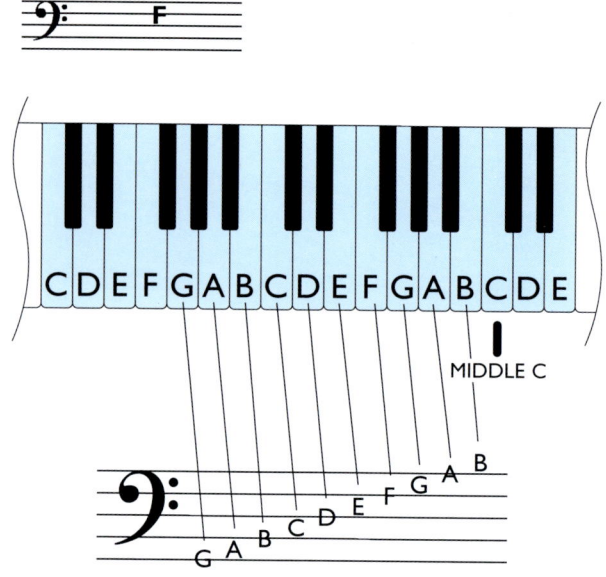

Left: This is the F below middle C, whose position on the stave is defined by the bass clef. The line on which it is written lies between the two dots on the clef (see notation at the top of the page).

INTRODUCING STAFF NOTATION

using 'the dots.' As you play it with your left and right hands, try to relate the keys you press to the written notes that correspond to them on the page. The fingerings you need for the scales appear above and below the two staves.

Left: The G being struck here by the left hand would appear on the lowest of the bass stave's five lines. The D on which the thumb lightly rests is notated on the middle line of the stave.

Above: Two hands and two Cs. The right hand thumb sounds middle C (the first treble stave note shown right), while the left hand's 5th finger plays the lower C that appears on the bass stave immediately after the vertical 'bar line.'

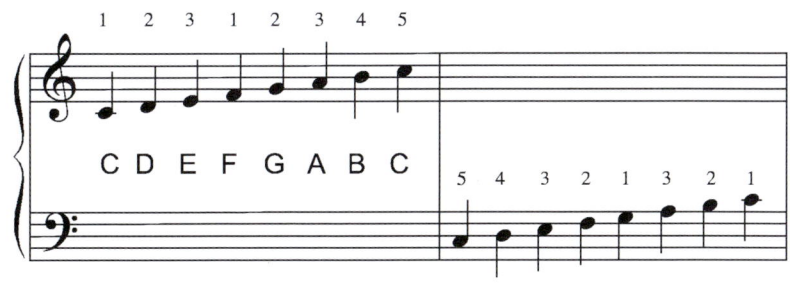

INTRODUCING STAFF NOTATION

Beats and bars

We've seen how staff notation is used to set down the pitches of the notes we want to play; now let's look at the way it handles another vital musical ingredient – rhythm.

Nearly all songs and instrumental pieces have a regular underlying pattern of pulses; a waltz, for example, consists of a recurring cycle of three beats (one strong, two weak – **1**-2-3, **1**-2-3), while a march is often made up of groups of four beats – with the strongest stress falling, once again, on the first of these (**1**-2-3-4, **1**-2-3-4). You can identify the pulse pattern of a written piece of music from the top figure of the 'time signature' that appears at its start. This usually corresponds to the number of beats in its rhythmic cycle – so a four-beat composition such as a march will have an upper figure of 4, and a waltz will be prefixed by a 3.

The time signature's lower figure is a kind of 'code number,' identifying the type of note that is going to be used to represent individual beats. Here's a table showing the most frequently encountered of these notes, and also giving their names and the numbers that stand for them; as you'll see, each successive note is exactly half the length of its predecessor.

Of the notes below, the quarter note (value = 4) is the one that most often 'stands for' a single beat. In a piece with a '4/4' time signature, the underlying pulse cycle is made up of groups of 4 quarter notes, and each of these 4-beat sections is written down on the stave in a **bar** – a horizontal space marked off with vertical lines.

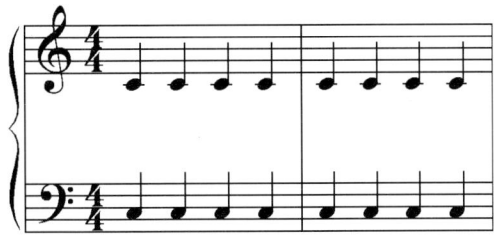

A composition in 3/4 time, by contrast, will have 3 quarter notes to the bar.

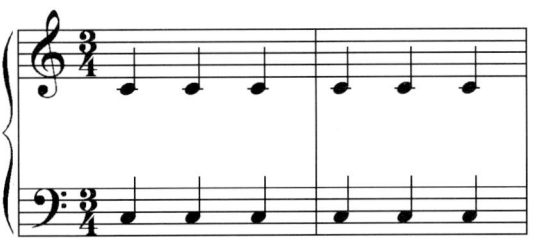

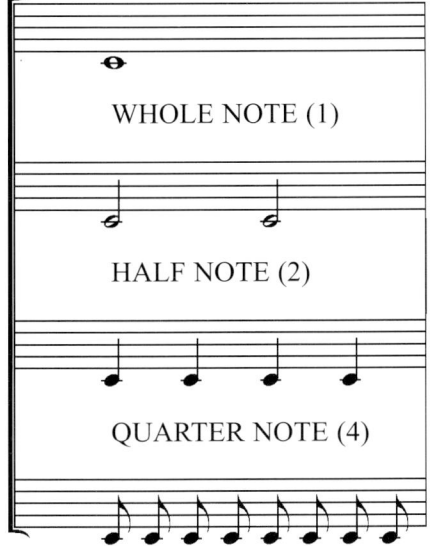

Right and opposite: The metronome seen here can be set to click (at any chosen speed) on individual beats, such as those represented by quarter notes in 4/4 and 3/4 time. The clear, indication of pulse it provides can be a very useful aid to practice – especially when learning pieces with a strong rhythmic content, as the girl in the photograph opposite appears to be doing!

How note lengths are shown with staff notation

Though it has a basic pulse defined by the number of beats to the bar, most music contains notes of varying durations (shorter and longer than the 'pulse' beat) – all of which can be written down using the symbols shown on the previous two pages.

In *Frère Jacques*, for example, the opening syllables all occupy single (quarter note) beats; notation for these, indicating pitch (the first note is middle C in the treble clef), lyrics, and rhythm, appears alongside. Try playing it with your right hand: as on page 49, fingering numbers are printed above each of the notes.

The quarter notes continue until we reach the 'vous' of 'Dormez vous?', at the end of bars 3 and 4: this lasts for two beats, and is therefore indicated by a half note.

On the next line, the four syllables 'Sonnez les ma-' have to fit into the first two quarter note beats of the bar. To notate these we use eighth notes, which can either appear with separate tails (as in the example on this page), or 'beamed' together into groups that 'add up' to one or two quarter note beats (as on page 53).

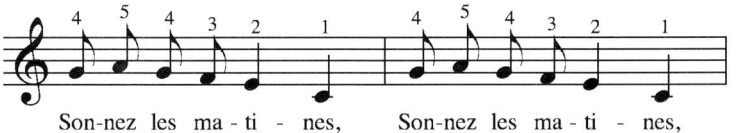

For the concluding bars of the song, with its 'bell' sounds, we need a combination of quarter notes and half notes.

INTRODUCING STAFF NOTATION

Left: The left hand starts to play bar 1 of *Frère Jacques*, with the 5th finger on the first C quarter note, and the 4th ready to sound D.

Below: We've now reached bar 5 of the tune, and the thumb strikes an eighth note A (the '-nez' of 'Sonnez les matines.')

Left: 'Ding' and 'dong'. The Cs (quarter notes and half notes) for these 'bell' sounds in bars 7 and 8 are produced by the left hand's 2nd finger.

Here's the complete tune of *Frère Jacques* again, this time set out in the bass clef, so that you can perform it with your left hand.

53

INTRODUCING STAFF NOTATION

Do Ye Ken John Peel – 1

*It's now time to use your new-found knowledge of 'the dots' to learn a new piece:
the traditional British song* Do Ye Ken John Peel.

You'll be playing it in the key of F, which, as you'll remember from pages 42-43, includes a black note, B flat. There are two ways of showing flats and sharps on the stave, one of which is simply to place a flat (♭) or sharp (#) symbol in front of a note. In the example below, the first whole note is a 'regular' B (sometimes called a 'B natural'), while the second one, prefixed by the flat sign, is a B flat.

This method becomes rather repetitious in a key like F, in which every B is normally flattened. A convenient shortcut is to insert a so-called 'key signature' just after the clef on each stave. This consists of one or more flat or sharp symbols, placed on the line or space corresponding to the note they apply to, and serving as an instruction to play every such note as a flat or sharp.

Left: The second of the two left hand note pairs shown in the notation on page 55. The 4th plays G, and the 2nd B♭. It's important to remember that the flat symbol in the key signature applies to all B♭s – not just the one on the second line from the bottom on the bass stave where the symbol actually appears.

We'll be using the F key signature throughout *John Peel* – but before getting to grips with the whole tune, let's focus on two of its elements. The first is the left hand accompaniment, featuring pairs of notes struck simultaneously. Here are six of them: look closely at the notation and photographs indicating their fingering, and then practice them slowly.

John Peel also presents a challenge to the right hand, which has to play two F notes lying eight notes (an **octave**) apart. The lower F is struck by the thumb, and the upper one by finger 5. Position your hand as shown below, and get used to the unfamiliar sensation (and the stretch!) as you sound the two Fs, one after the other.

Above: On the first quarter note of the second bar opposite, the left hand's 5th and 3rd fingers strike (respectively) C and E, as the 4th and 2nd prepare for the next notes (D and F).

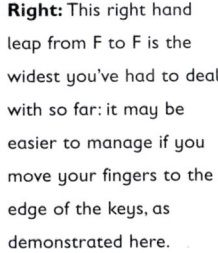

Right: This right hand leap from F to F is the widest you've had to deal with so far: it may be easier to manage if you move your fingers to the edge of the keys, as demonstrated here.

INTRODUCING STAFF NOTATION

Do Ye Ken John Peel – 2

These two pages contain the complete melody and accompaniment for Do Ye Ken John Peel.

You may initially be a little daunted by the proliferation of notes and bars – but take a closer look at the music, referring back, where necessary, to the explanations provided earlier in this chapter, and you'll soon begin to make sense of it.

The staves on which the notation appears carry treble and bass clefs, followed by a key signature (showing that all Bs should be flattened), and a 4/4 time signature indicating that the piece has an underlying pulse corresponding to a quarter note, and that there are four quarter note beats in every bar.

Above: On beat one of the second bar of *Do Ye Ken John Peel*, the right hand's 5th finger strikes a C quarter note, accompanied by F and A from the left hand's 5th and 3rd.

Left: Bar four, beat two: a B♭ in the treble, and D and F in the bass. Note how both hands are already moving into position to play the next notes (G in the right hand, C and E in the left).

56

INTRODUCING STAFF NOTATION

The clefs and key signatures recur at the start of every new line, but the time signature is written only once, at the start of the piece.

Suggested fingerings are given by the small numbers above the notes; between the staves are larger figures (1, 2, 3, 4) reminding you where the beats fall within the bars. The first three beats of the opening bar are actually silent, as the tune begins on its 4th beat. The little squiggly signs in the treble clef are quarter note 'rests' indicating that the right hand is silent during three-quarters of the first bar while the thick bar in the bass clef is a whole note 'rest,' indicating that the left hand is silent for the whole bar. But be sure to count '1-2-3' prior to starting the piece, in order to get the correct feel and establish a steady pulse.

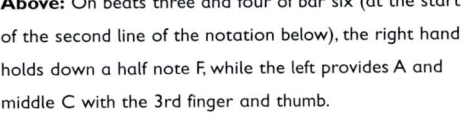

Above: Notes and their equivalent rests.

Above: On beats three and four of bar six (at the start of the second line of the notation below), the right hand holds down a half note F, while the left provides A and middle C with the 3rd finger and thumb.

Chapter 5

Co-ordinating your hands

In many piano pieces, including *Do Ye Ken John Peel*, the right hand supplies the melody while the left hand takes a supporting role by providing an accompaniment. Over the next few pages, though, we'll be exploring the musical possibilities and technical challenges that arise when your two hands are given more equal responsibilities. Being able to cope with comparatively complex treble and bass passages simultaneously is an essential part of playing the piano, and mastering the material in this chapter will give a valuable boost to your skill and confidence – and prepare you for the more demanding pieces that are still to come!

CO-ORDINATING YOUR HANDS

Leading with the left hand

Many melodies, as the great songwriter Richard Rodgers demonstrated in Do-Re-Mi *from* The Sound of Music, *are simply notes of a scale, reordered into more interesting patterns – and the same is true of the left hand bass figure (jazz or pop musicians might call it a **riff**) on which the following exercise is based.*

It's in the key of F, already familiar from *Frère Jacques* and *John Peel*. Back in Chapter 3 (pages 42-43), you learned the right hand version of a scale of F; try it now with your left hand, using the fingering shown here.

Next, we're going to select five notes from the scale – the two Fs, A, C, and D – and build them into the sequence set out in the notation opposite. Each of its eight 'steps' is a quarter note, and is fingered as it was in the full scale.

Left: The left hand's 3rd finger crosses over the thumb to reach the sixth note (D) of an ascending F major scale. The raised index finger is heading for the adjacent E that will be played next.

Left: Here, the 3rd finger strikes the D from our all-quarter note riff (F-A-C-D-F-D-C-A). As E isn't required, the thumb moves into position on F.

Keep the notes sounding smooth by holding down the keys you strike for as long as possible, releasing each of them only just before you move on to the next one. Once you can perform the figure steadily, and at a reasonable speed (with each quarter note beat lasting about a second or less), you'll be ready to add an accompaniment – provided, for a change, by the right hand. It consists of a three-note, whole note chord which is sustained for a bar at a time, helping to 'fill in the gaps' left by the faster-moving left hand.

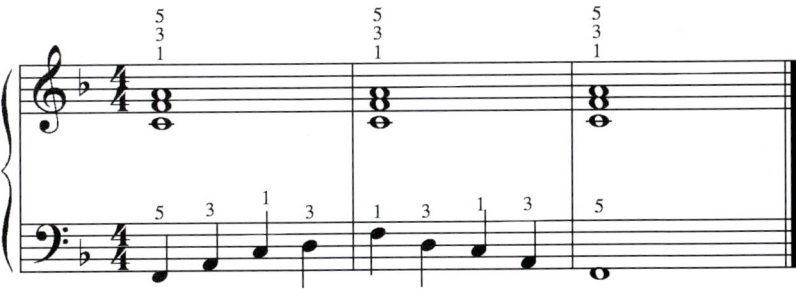

Above: This photograph shows the finger positions for beat three in bar 1 of the two-handed exercise notated opposite. The right hand is sustaining a whole note C-F-A chord with its thumb, 3rd, and 5th digits, while the left hand thumb plays a C.

Having got the feel of this, turn the page, and we'll try taking your left-hand riffing a stage further!

An extended bass riff

*The bass figure you've just learned begins on F – the so-called **root** of the scale of F to which it gives its name. It then skips up to A and C: each of these leaps, F-to-G-to-A and A-to-B flat-to-C, spans three note-names, and the **intervals** (to use a technical term) between them are therefore known as **thirds**.*

The next interval (C to D) is just one scale-step, while reaching the upper F from D involves another 'jump' of a third – before the pattern is reversed as we head back down to the lower F.

Let's see what happens when we apply this cycle of intervals to different starting-notes. In the following exercise, our riff commences not on F but on B flat; when playing it, use the same left-hand fingerings as you did for the original figure.

Next, try the same riff, shifted a step upward to start on C. Again, the fingerings are unchanged.

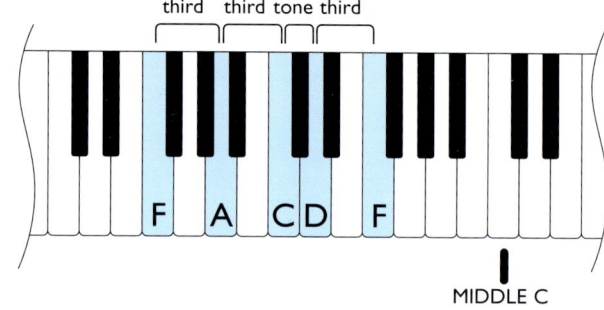

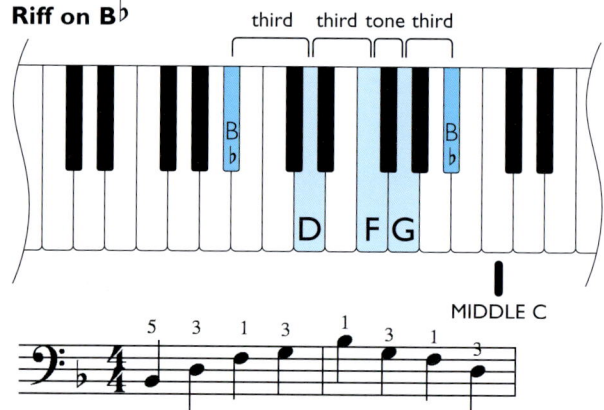

Above: The left hand's thumb reaches the higher of the two B♭s in the 'shifted' riff whose notation appears in the middle of the column next to the picture.

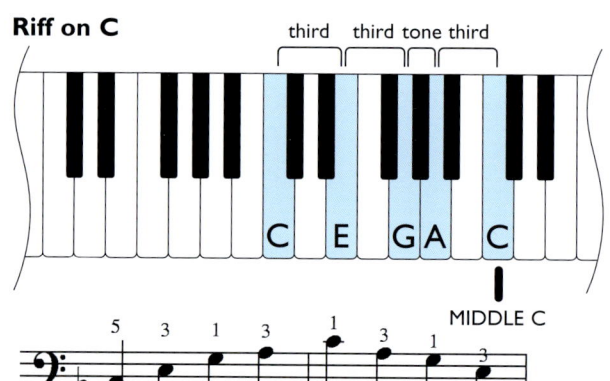

Playing the F, B flat, and C versions of the riff one after the other as shown below, and then returning to a variation of the F pattern at the end, creates a pleasing progression – especially when you combine it with the right hand chords indicated in the notation. Like the ones on the previous two pages, they're each made up of three notes; practice them on their own first, and then add the left hand when you feel confident!

Left: The third, C-based version of the riff climbs to middle C, which is struck by the thumb.

Right: The fingerings seen here could be used for beat 2 of either bar 2 or bar 8 of our nine-bar riff (shown above). The left hand 3rd finger sounds a D, while its thumb is positioned on the C immediately below. Meanwhile, the right hand provides a chordal backing playing C, F, and A.

CO-ORDINATING YOUR HANDS

Two-handed workouts

Your left hand fingers will be feeling supple (and maybe just a little tired!) after their exertions over the last few pages.

The remaining exercises and music in this chapter are going to make additional demands on them, though the technical challenges they present will be shared more equally with the right hand.

The 'busy' bass in our earlier riffing sequence was linked to a comparatively static treble – but you'll also be frequently confronted with pieces featuring simultaneous rapid movement in both their upper and lower parts. The best way to get your fingers and brain accustomed to these is to practice two-hand, scale-based passages – so here, to start with, is a bass-and-treble scale of C: something you've played before with separate hands, though it's much harder when you combine them. Take it slowly at first and gradually build up speed as you gain confidence.

Above: Here left and right hands play the third step (E) of the two-handed C scale notated below. The right hand thumb, en route to F, has just passed under the 3rd finger; simultaneously, finger 2 in the left hand is heading toward the F that lies an octave below.

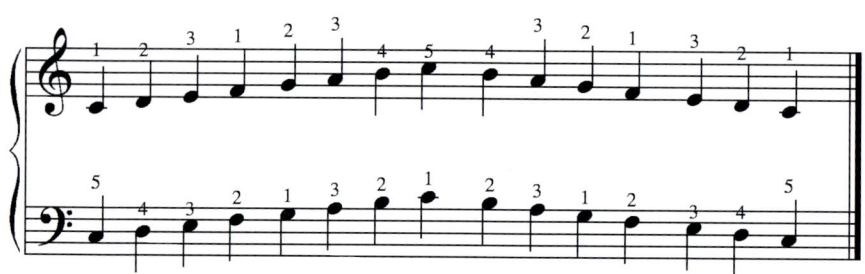

CO-ORDINATING YOUR HANDS

Now let's try the same scale in what's called **contrary motion**: initially, the right hand goes up the keyboard while the left descends; then the movement is reversed, with the right heading back down, and the left coming up. The fingerings are unaltered, and at the start and finish both thumbs meet on middle C.

Above: Moving your two hands along the keyboard in opposite directions will initially feel a little strange – but the sensation is also rather enjoyable! This photograph shows the second note of the contrary motion scale whose notation appears opposite.

Lastly, we have an exercise in which both hands 'share' parts of a scale; it looks easier than the previous ones, but the aim is to produce a seamless flow of notes, unaffected by the changeover of hands that occurs between middle C and D. Take it slowly at first, then see if you can speed it up without sacrificing clarity and articulation.

Left: In our 'shared' exercise, the right hand thumb sounds a D, taking up where the left (which has just played middle C) leaves off. This hand-to-hand switchover should be as smooth and unobtrusive as possible.

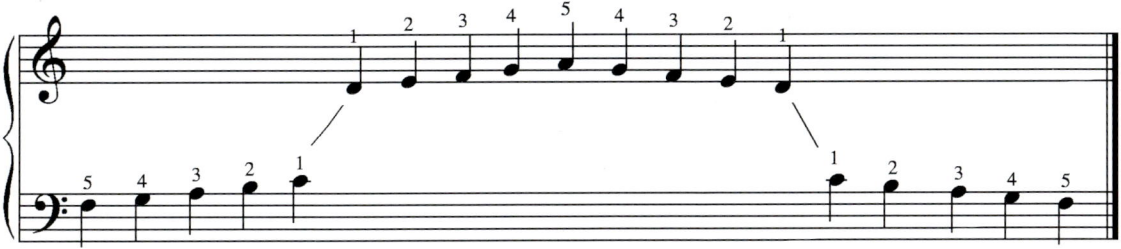

CO-ORDINATING YOUR HANDS

Tallis's canon

To put your hand-to-hand co-ordination to the test, here's an ingeniously constructed and beautiful melody written in the 16th century by the English musician Thomas Tallis.

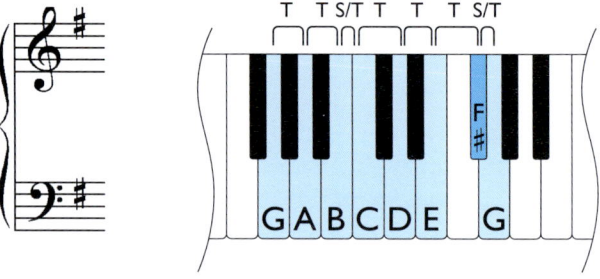

It's a **canon** – a type of composition in which a tune is designed to 'overlap' with itself. Nursery rhymes, such as *London's Burning* and our old favorite, *Frère Jacques,* can also be performed as canons, with one singer starting off, another taking up the opening line of the song as the first vocalist begins the second line, and so on…but *Tallis's Canon* is somewhat more sophisticated than either of these, and the time you spend learning to play it will be well worthwhile.

A single sharp

The piece is in the key of G, which we haven't used before. As you can see from the diagram and photograph opposite, the G scale is made up of seven white notes, and one black one – the F sharp that supplies its seventh, penultimate step. Consequently, the key signature for *Tallis's Canon* is a single sharp symbol (#) on the 'F' lines of the treble and bass clefs, reminding us to use F sharp, and not the white F natural key, throughout.

Above right: On beat 2 of the second full bar of *Tallis's Canon*, the right hand strikes an A while the left, which has just begun its rendition of the tune, plays an F#.

Right: The last beat of the canon's fifth full bar, featuring a D from the left hand thumb, and a B from finger 3 on the right hand.

CO-ORDINATING YOUR HANDS

The canon's rhythm is very simple: all the notes, except the final one, are quarter notes (of which there are four to a bar, as the 4/4 time signature tells us); but the fingering required is not always straightforward, especially in the left hand. Practice the tune slowly, with one hand at a time, and then combine the two strands of melody as indicated by the notation.

Above: Here we've arrived at the end of full bar 7. The right hand has reached its last few notes (it's currently playing the B on beat 4), but the left, on D, still has some way to go!

Chapter 6

Major and minor

All the scales and chords featured so far in this book have been so-called 'major' ones – but this chapter introduces you to their 'minor' cousins, which are differently constructed, and generate a distinctive, often melancholy, musical atmosphere. Their notes can be combined to create striking melodies and effects, as you'll discover when you tackle the traditional English tune *Greensleeves*, and they are also essential ingredients in blues, jazz, and many other popular music styles. Read on to learn more about what one great songwriter, Cole Porter, famously described in the lyrics to *Ev'ry Time We Say Goodbye* as 'the change from major to minor…'

Major and minor chords

The principal difference between 'major' and 'minor' scales lies in the spacing of the third of their eight 'steps:' in a major scale, the third step is two semitones (= a tone) above the second one, while the minor has a 'third' only a semitone higher than its 'second' (see diagram.)

The effect of this change can be heard clearly when we play chords incorporating the two different intervals. The notation shown below right displays a two-handed C major chord of a kind you've encountered several times before; it's followed by one of C minor, containing an **E flat** (see photograph) instead of the regular E (E natural) featured in its predecessor.

As you can see, the pitch of the altered note in the second chord is indicated by a 'flat' sign (♭) Flats and sharps placed in front of individual notes are known as 'accidentals,' and unlike the symbols shown in key signatures (which apply 'universally' throughout an entire piece), they only affect pitches of specific notes within the bar where they appear.

Scale steps:

```
           1/2  2/3
MAJOR      ⌣   ⌣
           T   T

MINOR      ⌣   ⌣        T = tone
           T   S/T      S/T = semitone
```

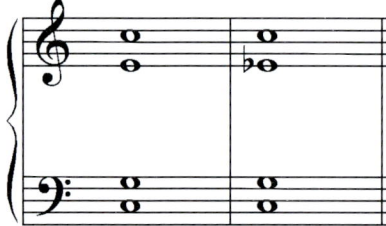

Right: This is the two-handed C minor chord that appears in the notation above the picture. The left plays a C and G, while the right sounds a second C with the 5th finger, plus the E♭ that gives the chord its 'minor' status.

MAJOR AND MINOR

Left: A four-note chord of F minor, as written on the staves below. It comprises F and A♭ (left hand) and F and C (right hand).

Below: Here, G minor — the second of the three chords in the accompanying notation — is being played, with G and B♭ in the right hand, and G and D in the left.

Let's try out some other majors and minors. Below is a chord of F major, similar to the ones you played in *Do Ye Ken John Peel* (see pages 54-57); it's followed by one of F minor, whose 'active ingredient' is the A flat marked out by the accidental.

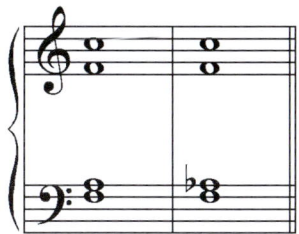

To finish, we have a bar containing both G major and G minor chords. The first of these is a major, with an unaltered B; the second is a G minor, with a B flat accidental; and the final chord is another G major, in which the B flat sign is canceled by a 'natural' symbol (♮) that instructs us to play the B in its regular, 'white note' form once again.

Harmonic minor scales

Minor keys have other unique characteristics in addition to their flattened thirds. Their scales, unlike those of majors, exist in two distinct forms, 'harmonic' and 'melodic,' and we'll focus first on the former.

The distances between the eight notes in a harmonic minor scale, and how they compare to a standard major's, are displayed in the following diagram.

```
                  Scale steps:
                 1/2  2/3  3/4  4/5  5/6  6/7  7/8
HARMONIC         ⌣    ⌣    ⌣    ⌣    ⌣    ⌣    ⌣
MINOR            T   S/T   T    T   S/T  3S/Ts S/T
MAJOR            ⌣    ⌣    ⌣    ⌣    ⌣    ⌣    ⌣
                 T    T   S/T   T    T    T   S/T
```

T = tone   S/T = semitone

Here now is the notation for a two-handed harmonic scale of A minor. Practice it with left and right hands separately before you try combining them.

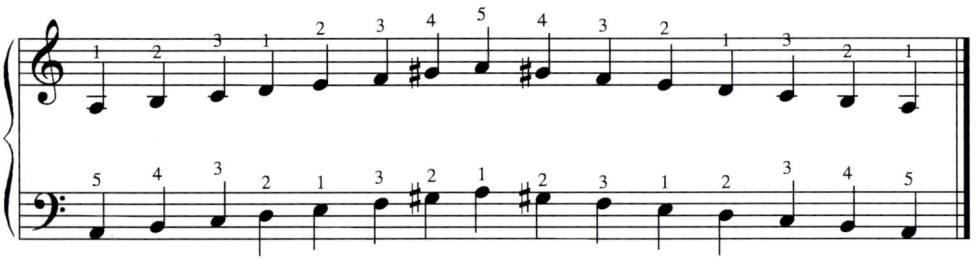

Above: The most striking feature of the harmonic minor scale is the three-semitone interval between its 6th and 7th steps – F and G# in A harmonic minor, fingered here by fingers 3 and 4 (right hand) and 3 and 2 (left).

Seven of this scale's eight notes are shared with that of C major; its one altered pitch is the sharpened penultimate step – a G#. Rather curiously, this ebony is always notated with an accidental, and not indicated in the key signature for A minor, which, like C major's, contains no sharps or flats.

The same convention applies to the 'sevenths' of all other minors, including the E harmonic minor shown below. This one is closely related to G major: both scales feature an F#, which appears in their key signatures, but the E minor scale's sharpened seventh (D#) is, once again, displayed only as an accidental.

Above: At the 'summit' of E harmonic minor: the left hand thumb and right hand 5th finger each play an E, while the 4th (right) and 2nd (left) position themselves on the D# a semitone below.

The final harmonic minor scale on these pages is one of D minor. It bears the same key signature as F major (a single B♭), but uses an accidental for its raised seventh step, C#.

Above: Step five (A) on an ascending scale of D harmonic minor. The next note will be B♭, struck by the 3rd finger on each hand; the left hand's 3rd finger has to cross over the thumb to reach it.

Melodic minor scales

Harmonic minor scales produce a distinctive, rather angular musical effect, but their 'melodic' variants are a little easier on the ear – though this pleasant sound comes at the expense of some technical complications, involving both the construction of the scales and the way they're notated.

As you can see from the diagram below, the first five notes of a melodic and harmonic minor are identical. The pitches of a melodic minor's sixth and seventh degrees depend on whether the scale is rising or falling: on its upward path, there's a gap of a tone between the fifth and sixth, and sixth and seventh steps, and then – as with the harmonic minor – a gap of a semitone separating its seventh and eighth notes.

Scale steps – ascending

	1/2	2/3	3/4	4/5	5/6	6/7	7/8
MELODIC MINOR	T	S/T	T	T	T	T	S/T
HARMONIC MINOR	T	S/T	T	T	S/T	3S/Ts	S/T

T = tone   S/T = semitone

Above: Sounding C# in a rising scale of E melodic minor (see notation at the top of page 75), with the hands separated by two octaves.

When the scale descends, however, the distance between its top note and the seventh step widens to a tone – and while the seventh and sixth degrees also have a tone between them, the sixth and fifth are just a semitone apart. The remaining spaces are unaltered.

Scale steps – descending

	8/7	7/6	6/5	5/4	4/3	3/2	2/1
MELODIC MINOR	T	T	S/T	T	T	S/T	T
HARMONIC MINOR (same when ascending or descending)	S/T	3S/Ts	S/T	T	T	S/T	T

T = tone   S/T = semitone

Below: The same scale, going downward: both hands strike D natural (its 7th step), and are ready to continue to C natural.

Accidentals are constantly required when writing out melodic minors on the stave. Above is shown a scale of E melodic minor for you to play; like its harmonic cousin, it has a single F# in its key signature, but in its rising form, its sixth and seventh degrees (C# and D#) have to be prefixed with sharp signs – which must then be canceled with naturals on the way down.

D melodic minor (whose harmonic version, like E minor's, you learned on pages 72-73) has a B flat in its key signature: this has to be made natural on the scale's upward path, and subsequently reinstated as B flat in the descending scale. C# and C♮ accidentals are also needed to give the correct pitches for the scale's rising and falling sections.

Left: The transition from B♮ to C# during the ascending half of the scale of D melodic minor. The Bs are played by the 3rd finger of each hand, while the C#s will be sounded by finger 2 (left) and finger 4 (right).

MAJOR AND MINOR

Greensleeves – 1

Though musical theoreticians make hard and fast distinctions between melodic and harmonic minors, elements of both can often be found in a single piece.

A classic example of this tendency to mix and match notes from the two types of scale is the celebrated old English tune *Greensleeves*, whose elegant twists and turns present us with a succession of accidentals, and whose accompaniment features a piquant combination of minor and major chords.

The version of *Greensleeves* on the next few pages is in A minor – a key which, as explained on pages 72-73, has many notes in common with its related major, C. Both C major and A minor share the same 'blank' key signature, with no sharps or flats; the *Greensleeves* melody, however, includes sharpened, as well as natural, Fs and Gs (respectively, the sixth and seventh steps of the A minor scale).

Here's its first, 16-bar section: it's in 3/4 time, with three quarter note beats to every bar. Begin by playing the right hand part by itself (because of the layout of the tune, the fingerings are not quite the same as those you've previously used for the A harmonic minor scale), then add the left hand 'backing' – a mixture of single bass notes and two- and three-part chords.

Above: The second beat of the second full bar of *Greensleeves*, with the right hand's 5th finger sounding F.

Right: We've now reached beat three of the piece's seventh full bar: the left hand plays D (5th finger) and B (thumb) to accompany the G# sounding in the melody.

MAJOR AND MINOR

Left: In the penultimate full bar, the left hand begins a rising sequence of notes starting on A; this is held down by its 5th finger, while the 3rd and 2nd position themselves on (respectively) C and E. Meanwhile, the right hand plays a half note A.

MAJOR AND MINOR

Greensleeves – 2

If you're familiar with other versions of Greensleeves, *you'll probably have realized that the rhythm of the opening part of the melody, as shown on pages 76-77, has been slightly simplified to place each of its moving notes directly on one of the three underlying quarter note 'pulses.'*

Most standard arrangements of *Greensleeves*, however, position some of these notes 'off the beat' – on the second half of a bar's second quarter note pulse. First, to remind yourself of the simpler rhythm, try playing Example 1 with your right hand, counting out the beats as indicated.

In Example 2, by contrast, the two eighth notes (E and F) in bar 2 subdivide the second beat, with the F falling – as it should – exactly half way between beat 2 and beat 3. The E immediately before it, though, sounds wrong: instead of striking it as a separate eighth note, as we just did, we need to lengthen the previous quarter note E so that it 'carries over' from beat one onto the first half of beat two. Such an 'extension' can be notated in two ways: either, as in Example 3, by joining the extra eighth note to the preceding quarter note with a **tie** (which warns the performer to treat the new note as a continuation of its predecessor, and not to strike it afresh)…or by placing a **dot** (musical shorthand for an instruction to extend any note by half its original duration) after the quarter note, as in Example 4.

Right: The F# in bar 2 of the *Greensleeves* notation opposite is played by the right hand's 4th finger; the left supports it with the notes of G and C.

The second section of *Greensleeves*, set out below in its two-handed form, uses dotted quarter notes, combined with eighth notes, to convey the tune's correct rhythm; you'll soon become accustomed to these, and will then be able to focus on synchronising your right and left hands, both of which face further challenges in the piece's final 16 bars!

Right: Bar 10 involves something of a stretch for the left hand, as it sounds two Cs, with a G 'sandwiched' between them. Simultaneously, the right hand's little finger strikes G, while its 4th prepares for the F# that comes next.

Chapter 7

Putting on the style

During the earliest stages of getting to grips with the keyboard, the emphasis is inevitably on the basics — finding and fingering the notes, co-ordinating your brain and your hands, and developing your ability to read staff notation. However, you've now reached the point where you should be thinking a little more about *how* you play, and starting to exploit your skills — and the capabilities of your instrument — in ways that will increase your musical satisfaction. Accordingly, this chapter explains how you can vary the sounds you make, expand the fairly limited palette of chords and rhythms you've so far been restricted to, and begin exploring the piano's almost unlimited stylistic capabilities.

The sustaining pedal

Except when they're actually being struck by their hammers, a piano's strings are usually prevented from vibrating by felt-covered dampers. These lift clear as the instrument's keys are pressed down to produce notes, but normally fall back into place, deadening the strings again, once the keys are released.

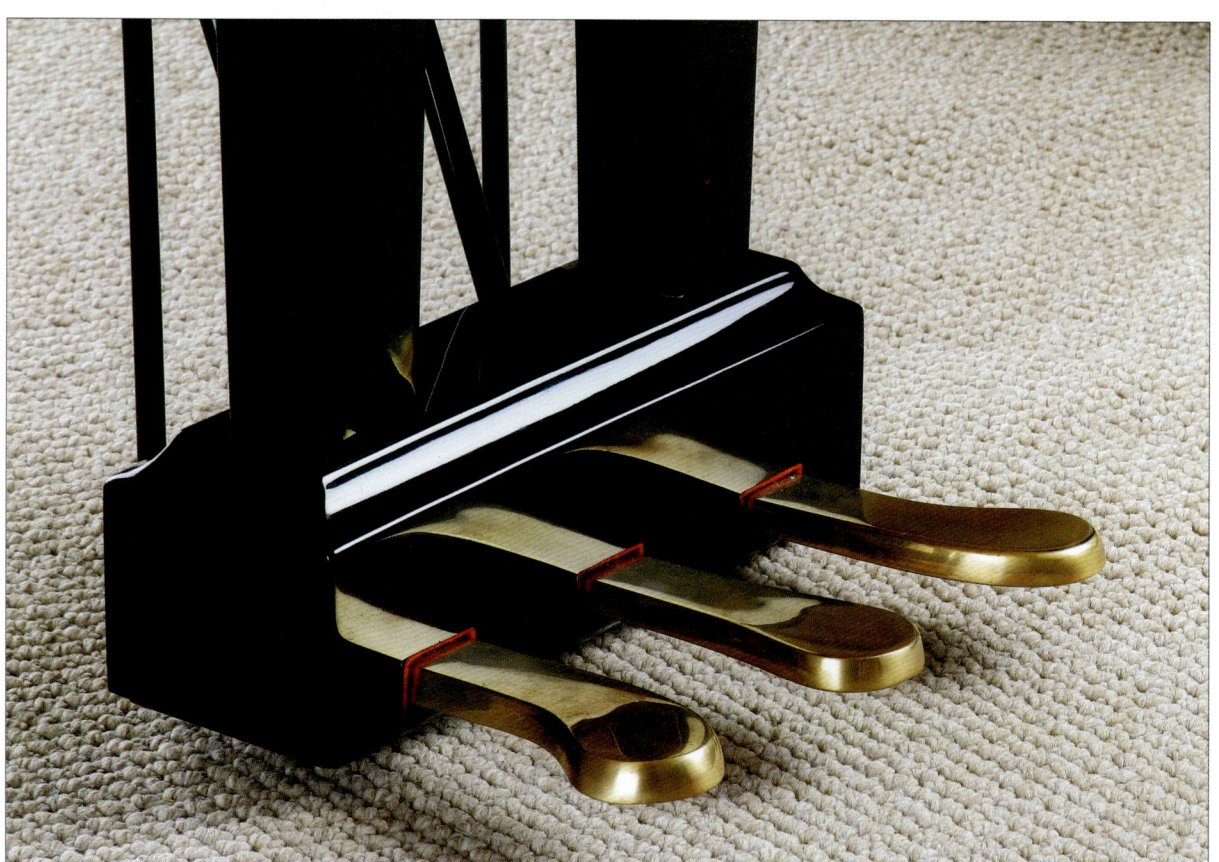

Above: The pedal unit of a grand piano. The sustaining pedal is on the right; beside it are the *sostenuto* and *una corda* pedals, whose functions are described on pages 84 and 85.

You can modify the action of the dampers via the **sustaining pedal** (frequently, but inappropriately, nicknamed the 'loud' pedal), the farthest to the right of the two (occasionally three) pedals fitted to an acoustic piano. Some digital keyboards offer an electronic simulation of the effect it provides, though on cheaper models the pedal unit itself may be a plug-in, optional extra.

Press the sustaining pedal down immediately after striking the notes or chords you want to sustain: it will open up all the piano's dampers, adding an impressive amount of extra resonance, but also blurring the notes you've already sounded into any others that are played while it's depressed. This can muddy the overall texture, and cause undesirable discords, so as a general rule, it's best to lift off the pedal

PUTTING ON THE STYLE

Left: This is the chord for the first beat of the opening bar of our exercise. The sustaining pedal can remain down throughout beats 1 and 2, as the notes they contain will sound good when blended together by the raised dampers.

Below: By lifting off the sustaining pedal at the precise moment when the fingers move to new notes, then pressing it down immediately afterward, we smooth over the inevitable interruption caused when the digits are raised, but avoid 'smudging' the sound.

at the moment you shift to fresh chords or notes, and then very quickly activate it again straight after striking these 'new' keys. Here's a simple exercise to help you get used to this technique: the 'Ped.' symbol and asterisk displayed beneath the bass stave indicate where you should press down and release the pedal.

The sustaining pedal is undeniably valuable, but many pianists don't appreciate how much it compromises the clarity of their tone when it's over-used. Always ask yourself if you really need to deploy it – and never allow it to become a substitute for smoothness of touch.

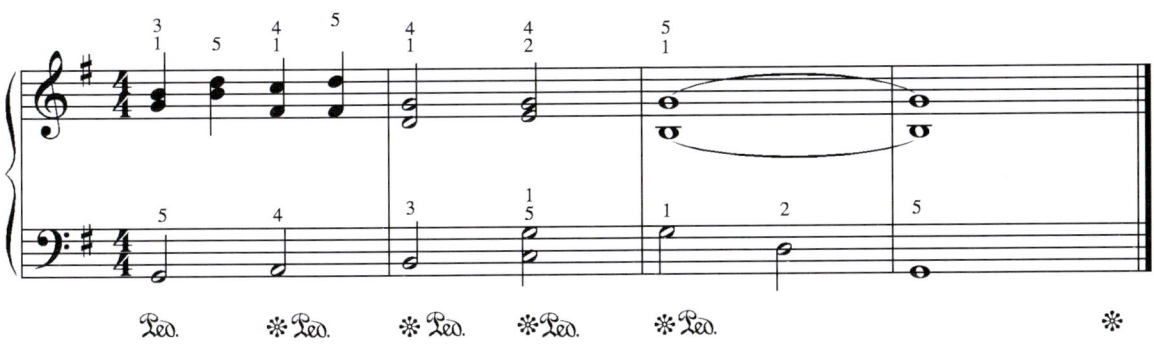

PUTTING ON THE STYLE

The 'soft' pedal and dynamic control

On pianos with three pedals, the center one serves as a 'selective' sustaining device: when activated after one or more keys are depressed, it keeps their associated string dampers raised for as long as the pedal is held down, but leaves all other notes unaffected. Named the sostenuto *pedal, and invented in the 19th century, it is now rarely used.*

The remaining pedal, mounted to the left of the regular sustaining pedal discussed earlier, is a more valuable tool. Popularly known as the 'soft' pedal, it's designed to facilitate quiet playing, and does so in one of two ways. On a grand piano, it shifts the instrument's hammers to one side, realigning them relative to the multiple strings that provide many of the instrument's notes, so that only two of a group of three strings, or one of a pair, are sounded. (This method of operation affects both volume and tone, and explains the pedal's original Italian name, '*una corda*' – single string.)

Upright pianos achieve similar results more simply: their soft pedals move the hammers closer to the strings, reducing the amount of power that even vigorous keyboard work can generate, but don't alter the overall sound as much as a true *una corda*.

The short piece shown opposite gives you the opportunity to practice your control of what musicians call dynamics: it starts and ends with some soft-pedaled chords, and builds to a loud climax at its half-way point. The changes in volume it incorporates are indicated by a series of notational symbols, which are explained in the table opposite.

Above and left: When the *una corda* pedal is depressed on a grand piano, the instrument's string-striking hammers move sideways…and so do its keys, which, of course, are linked to them. The center picture shows the top (treble) end of the keyboard in its normal position, without the pedal in operation. Note the gap between the top C key and the instrument's edge, which narrows noticeably (see lower photograph) once the *una corda* is activated.

PUTTING ON THE STYLE

Table of Dynamics

pp   pp - pianissimo (very quiet)

p   p - piano (quiet)

mp   mp - mezzo piano (moderately quiet)

mf   mf - mezzo forte (moderately loud)

f   f - forte (loud)

ff   ff - fortissimo (very loud)

           crescendo (get louder)

           diminuendo (get quieter)

Left: The 4-note D minor chord (D and A in the left hand, F and D in the right) from bar **1** of the notation above. While using the *una corda* as indicated by the markings beneath the bass stave, try experimenting with the sustaining pedal as well – its careful application will add to the impact of your changes in volume.

PUTTING ON THE STYLE

The 'three-chord trick'

One of the most useful skills a budding pianist can acquire is a practical understanding of the 'three-chord trick' – an elementary piece of theory that provides a valuable insight into the way many items of music (especially popular songs) are constructed.

Once you've grasped it, you'll find it much easier to locate chords, and combine them with melodies, in any key you choose.

To understand the three-chord concept, take a look at the scale of C major (right), and the chords set out beneath it. They are all majors, and their root notes are, respectively, the first (or eighth), fourth, and fifth steps of the scale: C, F, and G.

These three chords, officially termed the **tonic**, **subdominant**, and **dominant**, are the most extensively used of all harmonic accompaniments to simple melodies – and now you know the steps of the scale on which they're built, it's comparatively straightforward to find their equivalents in other keys. In F major, for example, the tonic is F, the subdominant B♭, and the dominant C; and chords with these roots perform exactly the same function for tunes in F major as C, F, and G do in C major.

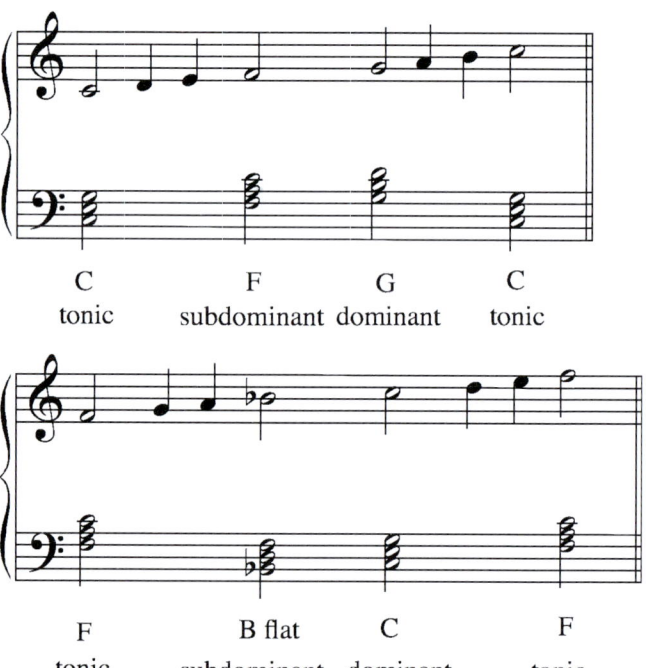

The most perennially popular three-chord trick-based musical form is the **12-bar blues** – a standard sequence of tonic, subdominant, and dominant harmonies, with a melody above it. Here's a blues in G major, where the three chords in question are, of course, G, C, and D. It's relatively plain and simple – but we'll soon be looking at ways in which it can be spiced up!

Right: Beat two of bar one in the blues notated opposite, with a low G whole note in the bass, and a quarter note B sounded by the right hand's 2nd finger.

PUTTING ON THE STYLE

Above and left: Bars 1-4 of this blues are largely rooted on the tonic (home key) chord of G major. In bars 5 and 6, the harmonic 'feel' shifts to the subdominant, C major, but returns to G for bars 7 and 8. The chordal center moves to D (the dominant) in bar 9, and to C in bar 10. The following bars are based around G (bar 11) and D (bar 12), before the piece comes to rest on its tonic chord.

12-Bar Blues (i): In bar four, the left hand strikes G and E on the third beat, while the right hand (silent at this point) prepares for the C in the next bar.

12-Bar Blues (ii): On the third beat of bar 11, the left hand's thumb and 2nd sound C and D together, producing a tasty 'clash.' The right hand sustains a D with the 5th finger.

PUTTING ON THE STYLE

Bluesy chords and syncopated rhythms

One of the important features missing from the 12-bar blues on the previous two pages is syncopation – *the shifting of rhythmical emphasis away from the 1-2-3-4 of the underlying quarter note pulse, and onto normally 'weaker' beats, that's an essential element of Afro-American music.*

Let's introduce some syncopated rhythms into the opening four bars of our blues. A combination of dots and ties, like those first seen on pages 78-79, is used to notate them – and to keep track of the 'displaced' accents, you may find it helpful to count out the eighth note subdivisions of the four quarter notes in each bar as you play the passage below.

Bars 1-4

We'll now 'jazz up' bars 5 to 8 with a little more syncopation (whose workings should be clear enough from the notation below) and some extra harmonic interest. The latter involves the addition of a slight discord (a B♭) to the C major subdominant chord in bar 5 – and then, during the next bar, the substitution of C minor for C major, as we replace the latter's E♮ with an E♭. Both these changes are regular tricks of the trade among jazz and blues artists.

Bars 5-8

PUTTING ON THE STYLE

Left: In bar 5, as the left hand holds down a C major chord combined with a B♭, the right hand begins a sequence of quarter notes and eighth notes (starting on C) that will take it to the very top of our 49-note keyboard!

Below: At the start of bar 9 (the first bar in the line marked 'final bars' that appears below), the two hands produce a dominant chord of D major, with an added C from the left's 2nd finger.

The fun continues during the last four bars, in which some further new notes find their way into the regular chords, and the bass line develops a life of its own!

After practicing the three 4-bar segments separately, try running them together to make a complete 12-bar blues.

Final bars

Right: An exciting leap in the penultimate bar of the 'final bars' section of our syncopated blues. Having just struck a low D with its little finger, the left hand heads for the C# nearly an octave above. The right is ready for the three-note final chord, due in two beats' time.

PUTTING ON THE STYLE

The Entertainer – 1

The 'ragtime' music of Scott Joplin (1868–1917) predates blues and jazz, but shares some of their rhythmic and harmonic characteristics – though it has a poise, elegance, and sophistication that are all its own.

We're going to conclude this chapter, and this book, with part of one of Joplin's best-loved compositions, *The Entertainer*, presented in a slightly simplified form.

The piece has four quarter notes to the bar, and is in D major: it's the first time we've featured this key, which includes two sharpened notes, F# (its third step) and C# (its seventh); as usual, these are displayed in its key signature. Here's a two-handed scale of D, and beside it are the 'three-chord trick' chords of D (tonic), G (subdominant), and A (dominant) that provide the harmonic 'bedrock' for Joplin's rag.

The right hand is responsible for *The Entertainer's* syncopated melody, while the left hand mostly supplies harmonic accompaniment in the form of quarter note chords and bass notes. The demands placed upon the hands are equal, but rather different; the left has to remain clear and steady, even when it's confronted with leaps like the ones shown below:

Meanwhile, the right hand needs to sound crisp and phrase smoothly as it picks out Joplin's famous tune:

PUTTING ON THE STYLE

Right: The left hand's thumb and little finger negotiate the distinctive B♭ to D interval in beats 3 and 4 of the second bar of the short excerpt from *The Entertainer*'s bass part that appears on page 90.

Left: The right hand tackles *The Entertainer*'s main theme: our photograph illustrates the last beat from the first full bar of the line of notation at the bottom of the opposite page, in which the thumb strikes F#, and the 5th finger D.

These examples will serve as useful warm-up exercises; once you've mastered the fingerings for them, turn the page, and prepare to tackle a complete, 20-bar section of *The Entertainer*.

Right: Another characteristic part of Scott Joplin's melody. The right hand's 2nd finger has just sounded the E eighth note on the fourth beat of bar 2 in the page 90 notation; its 3rd now plays F natural, while its 4th moves onto the F# that forms the first note of the next bar.

PUTTING ON THE STYLE

The Entertainer – 2

The Entertainer begins with a single-bar phrase played twice (in different octaves) by the right hand, and 'answered' by a left-hand figure that takes in an exotic-sounding 'alien' note, B♭, on its way down to a bass A.

Next comes a two-handed chord of A major (the dominant of the piece's key of D), preparing us for the main theme that's about to follow.

The tune itself consists of four phrases, each lasting approximately four bars (see brackets above notation). Notice how, after the first phrase ends with the tonic chord of D, the second one concludes on the dominant A. The slightly unsettled, 'up-in-the-air' atmosphere this creates is resolved by a return to the home key in the final two phrases, and throughout the melody Scott Joplin subtly varies his harmonies, using altered chords quite similar to the ones we encountered in our 12-bar blues on pages 88-89.

Learning *The Entertainer* will take a good deal of persistence; take it very slowly at first, and avoid using the sustaining pedal until you can finger the tune and backing reasonably smoothly. The piece doesn't require very much variation in volume, though a few *crescendos* and *diminuendos* (the Italian terms used by musicians as instructions to louden and soften the sound) are indicated. As you play, strive for steadiness, balance, and clarity, and you'll be sure to satisfy your listeners as well as yourself.

Right: The piece's short opening section concludes with a four-note A chord (see last bar of notation on this page). After striking this, lift your fingers abruptly off the keys in order to produce what musicians call a *staccato* effect.

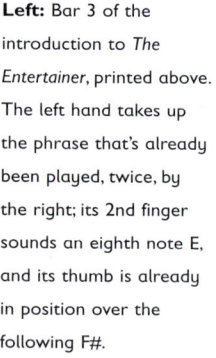

Left: Bar 3 of the introduction to *The Entertainer*, printed above. The left hand takes up the phrase that's already been played, twice, by the right; its 2nd finger sounds an eighth note E, and its thumb is already in position over the following F#.

Right: The last beat of full bar 7 is shown here. The eighth note D (right hand, 3rd finger) is supported by a three-note left hand chord comprising G#, D, and E.

Epilog – taking it further

You should be pleased with the progress you've made with your piano playing so far – and having reached the end of this book, it's time to plan the next stages in your journey of musical discovery.

When doing so, it's worth considering what styles of pianism – and music in general – most appeal to you. Do you have a favorite composer or songwriter? Is there a specific keyboardist you particularly admire? If so, try studying recordings of their work while following the notation for it, then select one or two of the simpler items on your playlist to learn yourself. In many cases, you'll be able to find books containing easy piano arrangements of the compositions that interest you: Internet-based stores offer the most extensive stocks of these, and your local library may also have a collection of printed music from which you can borrow. Initially, it will take some time to master even a comparatively straightforward piece – but the combination of listening, careful scrutiny of the dots, and (of course) painstaking practice will eventually pay dividends.

If this seems too daunting, you may prefer to seek out a sympathetic teacher who can guide you toward your goals, and help you overcome the technical challenges you encounter along the way. Consult your local music shop, or check out advertisements online and in the press, to find someone suitable: a good starting point is the list of US piano teachers, sorted by

Left: Practice and commitment will help you achieve your musical goals – and eventually enable you to unlock the mysteries of complex, eighth note-filled-pieces like the one on the stand of this grand piano!

Left: A good teacher – or a more experienced friend or relative willing to provide musical and technical advice – can be a source of inspiration to budding pianists.

state, provided on the Music Teachers National Association website (https://members.mtna.org/mtnareports/Teacher_Lookup.asp).

It's essential to develop your knowledge of musical theory as well as the practicalities of keyboard technique; several excellent beginners' guides to this subject are available, and, with their assistance, your grasp of the finer points of harmony and rhythm will keep pace with the steady growth of your playing skills. Meanwhile, for news on the latest in electronic keyboards, MIDI, and other cutting-edge aspects of musical technology, keep an eye on the articles and advertisements in magazines such as *Sound on Sound*, which are full of useful information.

Have fun as you learn and practice, and you'll be sure to derive years of pleasure from your piano or keyboard!

Index

accompaniment 6, 21, 31, 35, 36, 42, 55, 56, 58, 60, 76, 86
backing 6, 7, 38, 63, 76, 92
bar 49, 50-51, 52, 55, 56, 57, 61, 63, 66, 67, 70, 71, 75, 76, 78, 79, 81, 85, 86, 87, 88, 89, 90, 91, 92, 93
bass clef 48, 53, 56, 57, 66
beat 50-51, 52, 56, 57, 61, 63, 66, 67, 76, 78, 83, 86, 87, 89, 91, 93
black keys 21, 22, 26, 33, 40, 42
blues 69, 86, 87, 88, 89, 90, 92
canon 66, 67
chord 6, 14, 24, 33-43, 45, 61, 63, 69-79 86-89
chromatic scale 40, 41
classical music 6
computer 14, 19
contrary motion 65
crescendo 85, 92
Cristofori, Bartolomeo 10
crossover 34
dampers 18, 82, 83, 84
diminuendo 85, 92
dominant 86, 87, 88, 89, 92
dot 45, 48, 49, 54, 78, 79, 88, 94
Do Ye Ken John Peel 54-57, 59, 71
dynamics 84, 85
eighth note 50, 51, 52, 57, 78, 79, 88, 91, 92, 93, 94
electronic keyboard 6, 9, 14, 15, 19, 82, 95
E-mu Xboard 14, 19
Entertainer, The 90-93
Ev'ry Time We Say Goodbye 69
exercise 25, 26, 36, 60, 61, 62, 64, 65, 83, 91
fingering 24, 28, 30, 31, 32, 36, 38, 40, 42, 43, 49, 52, 53, 55, 60, 62, 63, 65, 67, 76, 81, 91
flat 42, 54, 62, 63, 70, 71, 75, 76
forte 85
fortissimo 85
Frère Jacques 28-31, 34, 42-43, 52, 53, 60, 66
Greensleeves 69, 76-79
half note 51, 52, 57, 75
hammers 10, 12, 82, 84

harmonic scales 72, 73, 74, 76, 86, 87, 88, 90
harpsichord 10
interval 40, 62, 70, 72, 90
jazz 6, 60, 69, 88, 90
Joplin, Scott 90, 91, 92
keys 6, 10, 14, 15, 18, 19, 21, 22, 24, 25, 26, 28, 30, 33, 34, 36, 40, 42, 43, 46, 47, 55, 60, 72, 82, 83, 84, 86, 92
key signature 54, 55, 56, 66, 70, 72, 73, 75, 76, 90
ledger line 47, 49
loudspeaker 14, 15
lyrics 28, 52, 69
maintenance 16, 18
major chord 60, 68-79, 86, 88, 89, 90, 92
melodic scales 72, 74-75
melody 6, 21, 26, 28, 31, 33, 38, 43, 56, 59, 60, 66, 67, 69, 76, 78, 86, 90, 91, 92
mezzo forte 85
mezzo piano 85
middle C 22, 23, 25, 26, 28, 30, 31, 34, 35, 36, 37, 38, 39, 40, 42, 43, 46, 48, 49, 52, 57, 63, 65
MIDI (musical instrument digital interface) 19, 95
minor chord 68-79, 85, 88
Music Teachers National Association 95
natural 54, 66, 70, 71, 74, 75, 76, 91
organ 10
pedal 24, 82, 83, 84, 85, 92
pianissimo 85
piano
    acoustic 6, 14, 15, 18, 82
    baby grand 12
    concert grand 10, 12, 18, 19
    electronic 15
    forte 10
    grand 9, 10, 12, 13, 16, 18, 82, 84, 94
    upright 9, 10, 12, 13, 16, 18, 24, 84
piano strings 10, 11, 13, 18, 19, 82, 84
pitch 13, 18, 19, 22, 26, 30, 40, 46, 47, 48, 50, 52, 70, 74, 75
polyphony 16
pop music 6, 58
Porter, Cole 69

pulse 50, 51, 52, 56, 57, 78, 88
quarter note 51, 52, 53, 55, 56, 57, 60, 61, 66, 76, 78, 79, 86, 88, 89, 90
ragtime 90
rhythm 6, 45, 50, 51, 52, 67, 78, 79, 81, 88-89, 90, 95
riff 60, 61, 62-63, 64
Rodgers, Richard 60
Roland 15
root notes 33, 40, 42, 62, 86, 87
sample 9, 14, 15, 19
scales 32-43, 45, 46, 68-79
semitone 40, 41, 42, 43, 70, 72, 73, 74
sharp 42, 54, 66, 70, 72, 75, 76, 90
sostenuto pedal 82, 84
Sound of Music, The 58
Sound on Sound magazine 95
staccato 92
staff notation 6, 44-57, 81
stand, keyboard 16-17, 94
stave 46-47, 48-49, 51, 54, 56, 57, 71, 83, 85
Steinway, Henry E. (& Sons) 10
stool, music 13, 16-17, 22, 24
subdominant 86, 87, 88
sustaining pedal 82-83
syncopated rhythm 88-89, 90
synthesized sounds 9, 14, 19
Tallis's Canon 66-67
thirds 62, 72
'three-chord trick' 86, 90
tie 78, 88
time signature 50, 51, 56, 57, 67
tone 6, 10, 14, 24, 40, 68, 74, 83, 84
tonic 86, 87, 90, 92
transposing a tune 42, 43
treble clef 46, 52, 57
tune 6, 18, 19, 21, 24, 26, 28, 33, 34, 40, 53, 55, 57, 66, 67, 69, 76, 79, 86, 90, 92
tuner 18, 95
tuning 18, 19
una corda pedal 82, 84, 85
white keys 21, 22, 24, 26, 27, 30, 36, 40, 46
whole note 50, 54, 57, 61, 86
Yamaha 15
Yamaha CLP Clavinova 15